ON WINGS OF

Praise

*How I
found
real joy
in a
personal
friendship
with God.*

ON WINGS OF

Praise

KAY RIZZO

REVIEW AND HERALD® PUBLISHING ASSOCIATION
HAGERSTOWN, MD 21740

This book was
Edited by Penny Estes Wheeler
Designed by Patricia S. Wegh
Cover illustration by E. Blashfield
Cover illustration handtinted by Mary Rumford
Typeset: 13/14 Cochin

PRINTED IN U.S.A.

00 99 98 97 96   5 4 3 2 1

Library of Congress Cataloging in Publication Data
Rizzo, Kay D., 1943-
     On wings of praise: how I found real joy in a personal friendship
with God/Kay Rizzo.
          p.   cm.
     1. Rizzo, Kay D., 1943-   . 2. Seventh-day Adventists—
United States—Biography.   3. Spiritual biography—United States.
4. Christian life—Seventh-day Adventist authors.   I. Title.
BX6193.R58A3   1996
286.7'092—dc20
[B]   95-49789
                                                                    CIP

ISBN 0-8280-1050-1

DEDICATION

Thank You, Holy Spirit,
for doing everything
the Father and the Son promised
You would do.

ACKNOWLEDGMENTS

To the women I've met at women's ministry conferences across North America, thanks for planting the seeds for this book.

Penny Estes Wheeler, thank you for watering the ground with your encouragement.

Thanks, Kelli Wheeler and Rhonda Ringering, for adding fragrant blossoms to these principles of praise.

And to Ann Miller, thanks for articles, poems, and stories that enrich the soil.

To Connie Krueger, thank you for listening and responding to my ramblings, and not giving up on me.

And to my ever-present "lion of a man" who loved me during the most painful of growing times, I love you more than I could ever have imagined possible.

CONTENTS

Preface ∼ 11

CHAPTER 1 I Hate Religion ∼ 13

CHAPTER 2 Playing Church ∼ 23

CHAPTER 3 No Toy Boxes in Prison ∼ 27

CHAPTER 4 Lifting the Lid ∼ 37

CHAPTER 5 A New Song ∼ 49

CHAPTER 6 Living in the Perspective of Praise ∼ 63

CHAPTER 7 Daddy Dearest ∼ 71

CHAPTER 8 The Promise of Praise ∼ 83

CHAPTER 9 Healing and Praise ∼ 95

CHAPTER 10 Moving On ∼ 103

CHAPTER 11 Claiming My Inheritance ∼ 109

CHAPTER 12 The Bold and the Beautiful ∼ 117

CHAPTER 13 The Key Ring ∼ 125

CHAPTER 14 Power Tools of Victory ∼ 133

CHAPTER 15 The Perfect Woman I Want to Be ∼ 141

CHAPTER 16 God's Barbie Dolls ∼ 151

CHAPTER 17 Getting Real With God ∼ 161

Good news! God isn't playing games. He didn't send His Son to die on this pitiable planet so people could play Holier Than Thou Leapfrog, Mary Martyr, and Pin the Tale on the Heretic.

The Father didn't sacrifice the life of His beloved Son to enable a bunch of bearded fishermen to organize an elite social club, either. The King of the universe didn't grant salvation to humans so they could invent another religion, one with its very own game board and endless list of rules. God didn't provide the gift of eternal life so we could have a new toy box in which to "play."

"For God so loved . . ." Whether 2,000 years ago, 100 years ago, or today, God isn't looking for players to enhance His sporting pleasure. He is calling daughters who crave reality, sons who have had their fill of spiritual charades, children who yearn for truly transformed lives.

While many religious books lead the reader to a new life in Christ, and many discuss the rewards promised in the sweet by and by, *On Wings of Praise* tells a personal story of true joy found while living in the messy here and now. But this book's purpose is not to regale you with tales of what I and others may have done for God. Instead it contains true stories of what God can do in the lives of everyday people. Come. Journey with me on an adventure to end all adventures.

Remember being 10 or 11 years old and aching to grow up so you could do the things grown-ups do? This book is about growing up spiritually. It's about refusing to remain trapped in a spiritual toy box of one's own making, and leaving behind the childish game of *playing* church to become the person God created you to be. It's about becoming a blue-ribbon champion for the cause of God, about marching out to face the fearsome foe, about confidently displaying the armor of faith, truth, and love.

The soaring heights and incredible depths of the Holy Spirit's power aren't for spiritual infants. When we age physically and pass our energy peak, we expect to slow down. However, like all of God's other principles, the process of maturing is upside down and backward to what people expect. As we "age" spiritually, the pace of growth accelerates.

We receive a new quality of joy—a joy that comes from *knowing* God keeps His word and having confidence that He is managing all of our life. The possibilities are unbelievable when we choose to stop playing games and get real with God.

Warning! This incredible joy is highly explosive. It will blow the top off our comfortable little toy box, and the shrapnel of God's love will rain onto your entire world.

I Hate Religion

Don't talk to me about religion. I hate religion!" Cathy's eyes flashed with fury and her hands knotted with rage. "My father always quoted the Bible before beating me. 'Spare the rod,' he said, 'and spoil the child.' Scars and broken bones are all I have to show for all his religion."

The distraught teenager flailed one hand into the air. "The sooner I break free of my father's ironfisted religion, the happier I'm going to be. I hate religion and everything about it."

Cathy's words shocked me. Hate religion? How can that be? Like so many others who've grown up in the safety of the church, my entire existence was interlinked with religion. My church affiliation identified who I was. From the first time I toddled up to the flannel board in the children's department at my childhood church in Troy, New York, and placed a red flannel heart beside the picture of Jesus, I knew where I belonged. From the time I first lisped the words to the chorus "Into My Heart," the church was my life.

At age 10 I made my decision for Christ during a tent camp meeting at Union Springs, New York. Because there was no children's program that evening, my parents insisted I attend the adult meeting with them. I don't remember what topic the radio evangelist H.M.S. Richards presented that night. But at the end of the service he gave an altar call. And my response to that call determined the direction of my life forever.

The battle I fought that night was as genuine as any of the battles my adult counterparts were fighting. Finally I knew I could sit no longer. Regardless of the consequences, I had to go forward. My heartbeat thundered in my ears as I rose to my feet and made my way down to the front of the tent.

When school started that fall, our local pastor, Elder Robbins, asked me if I would like to attend a baptismal class. I eagerly agreed. The week before my baptism I composed a list of my top 10 worst sins. I figured that once I was baptized I'd have them all checked off in two weeks or less.

That didn't happen. My knees developed calluses as I struggled, simultaneously, to overcome and to hide my sin list from the world. I attended Christian schools, and whenever an altar call was made I was one of the first to acknowledge my need. I would leave the meeting feeling clean and new, and vowing, "This time it will be different—this time, God, I am going to be the best Christian ever," only to begin the game again the next morning.

Desperate to be deemed perfect in the eyes of God and the world, I played all the games. I recited the right texts. I sang the right songs and joined the right clubs. I passed out literature. I visited nursing homes and sang to the patients. After earning a Jasper Wayne award in my senior year of academy for raising money for missions, I expected to feel the exhilaration of perfection. It didn't come. A day or two later I broke the school rules by kissing Dan out behind the cafeteria. I cried myself to sleep that night, certain I was and would be lost forever.

I remember the day my Bible teacher drew a staircase on the chalkboard. "When we do what is right, it's like climbing steps toward perfection. Some of you are on step 1 while others of you may have reached step 10. At the end of your life, Jesus will look at your progress, and if you've been moving continually in an upward direction, His righteousness will make up for the gap that still exists between Him and you."

"Why work so hard, then?" I asked, 10 percent in jest, 90 percent in earnest.

"Because God will evaluate your performance before granting you His grace," my teacher replied.

Questions swirled in my brain. *Does God have to grant some people more grace than others? How can I know if I'm doing enough to warrant His grace?*

At our junior-senior picnic two of our senior guys drowned a month before graduation. Everyone talked about the boys as if they were saints, but we all knew better. They'd spent more time than they should with the girls out behind the cafeteria. They'd broken numerous rules. *Had they climbed enough steps to be granted that extra portion of grace needed for heaven?* I wondered.

I hobbled along until graduation, then went into a spiritual tailspin, a trial separation from my God. I indulged in cherry Cokes at the local teen hangout. I wolfed down hamburgers at the White City Diner. I allowed my 28-year-old boss to drive me home from work, knowing more was on his mind than my job performance. But God didn't give up on me. By the time fall came and I enrolled in college, I'd decided to give religion another chance. *Maybe if I become a missionary I can prove to Him that I'm really trying.* I renewed my childhood resolve to serve God overseas, preferably in India. Yet for all my good intentions, for all my resolve to "talk the talk," I stumbled and fell whenever I tried to "walk the walk." Battered and bleeding, I'd crawl to my feet once more, trying to hide the rips and the smudges in the "robe of Kay's righteousness."

Whenever spiritual exhaustion overwhelmed me, I rebelled. I resented the pressures I felt to "perform and conform." But somehow I'd always be lured back into the deadly game, knowing all the while how filthy, evil, and helpless I really was. I played the game in fear—fear that I'd do all the right things, sing all the right songs, and still miss out on eternity by one stair step. Adulthood and accompanying tragedies intensified my desire to earn my crown of righteousness. I became a hard-core religionist. I had to make it. If I failed . . . No, I couldn't fail. Not after I lost three beautiful babies. I had to make it if I expected to enjoy them in God's perfect world.

While the details may vary, my experience is not unique. Quite the contrary, my story is all too common and, some may say, hardly needs telling. Or does it? Christian women growing up in the protective custody of the church can relate to my quest for the heart of God. Like me, many have never experienced a dramatic victory over evil. No laser beam of truth zapped me while I traveled the road to Damascus, Pennsylvania, or to Portland, Oregon. There'd been no defining moment when the booze-soaked mind of a prodigal daughter cleared enough to recognize the beauty of God's abundant love. My raciest fantasy was to run away to New York City and become a Broadway singer. Too much common sense and my all-too-average musical ability prevented that tragedy.

Realistically, I knew I would move square by square across the game board—high school, college, marriage, and one day, teaching school—hardly a life of wantonness from which to be saved. No, the nasty little habitual sins I treasured would never make good reading for either the New York *Times* best-seller list or for the seeker after truth.

Like the Scripture-quoting, Bible-toting religionists of Christ's day, I knew the way to salvation. Game masters all, these men and their forefathers created a religion full of rules and restrictions, a game of dexterity and deception. And if points were given for effort, I could give a faithful Pharisee a run for his shekels. I knew that my Lord's most scathing rebukes were directed at the religionists of His day. Yet I didn't consider myself one, not really.

Don't misunderstand me. Intellectually, I believed that only through faith in Christ and Christ alone could I be made righteous. I read all the books, listened to the cassette tapes, attended the meetings, and could spout the jargon with sincerity and accuracy. But my heart, my innermost being, the Kay that King David wrote about in Psalm 139:13, the Kay hidden from all earthly eyes, continued to miss the point. Like it or not, I was a religionist toying with my salvation. And the longer I played, the more I hated the game and the more I wanted to escape.

~

Recently I heard the following truism: *Religion is what humanity tries to do for God, while Christianity is what God did and is doing for humanity.* Tell me, what good has "religion" done for society other than pit human beings against each other? Unbelievers are quick to remind us that millions have died in the name of religion. The first religious conflict began between Abel and his brother, Cain. And the slaughter goes on in places like Bosnia, Rwanda, Somalia, and South and Central America. It screams out at us from the placards of hate paraded in front of abortion clinics and from the sidewalks surrounding the White House.

A cynic described the variety of world religions as burger franchises. Whether McDonald's or Wendy's, Burger King or Jack-in-the-Box, flame-broiled or grilled, take your choice. The meat's the same; only the toppings vary to please individual taste buds. And whenever one's spirituality becomes a creed to follow or a set of rules to keep instead of a living, growing relationship that description is right.

Jesus Christ came to set His people free from the steel bands of religion imprisoning His people. He came not to set up a new religion for His children, but to establish a personal, loving, trusting relationship with them. He came to live out the will of the Father.

"What must I do to be saved?" a sincere young politician asked Christ.

The Master replied, "Keep the commandments."

The man searched his heart, but found no fault. He'd obeyed all the rules since childhood. He'd conscientiously honored his parents. He'd kept the Sabbath with great precision.

He'd stalwartly refused to covet his neighbor's curvaceous young wife.

Jesus' reply stunned the young man, and he "went away sorrowful: for he had great possessions" (Matthew 19:22). If this concerned politician, who so rigorously kept the laws, blew it, then what hope was there for me? I had no wealth to leave behind; I had no inheritance to forsake. Yet the similarities disturbed me. We were both playing the perfection game by the rules and not living it by the heart.

I'd like to think that the story didn't end there. Perhaps, after the Crucifixion, after Christ's resurrection, perhaps on the day of Pentecost or during one of Paul's travels, this young man discovered the truth Jesus tried to reveal to him that day. Perhaps he became one of the faithful deacons in the early Christian congregation. Perhaps God gave him time. Perhaps . . .

Recently I received a letter from Janette, a young friend of mine and a pastor's wife. "Kay," she wrote, "I'm so bored with playing church. The life has gone out of my experience. Every week I have to whip myself into an attitude of happiness. And on the way home I sink even lower into the pit of despair. This can't go on. Please help me to know what to do."

I've seen this same emotional exhaustion in the eyes of numerous Christian women across the country, women teetering on the paper-thin crust of spiritual burnout. The number of women who seriously have considered suicide as the only way out is chilling. The most desperate stories come from middle-aged pastors' wives trying to be the conciliatory buffer between their minister husbands and their adult children, and still maintain their own spiritual balance.

When asked if they are certain of their salvation, I detect a hesitancy in their voices, the same hesitancy I experienced for so many years.

One carefully groomed, 50-something woman told me of how she'd held a loaded gun to her head and counted to three, only to pull the trigger and discover the safety latch was still on. Another told me she was so depressed at one point that she sat in her car at a railway crossing longing to speed into the path of the oncoming train. She actually had to lift her foot off the gas pedal with her hands to keep from accelerating onto the railroad tracks and certain death.

I knew that my friend Janette had recently gone through a period of severe censure delivered by fellow church members for little more error than youthful enthusiasm. Psychologists tell us that burnout, spiritual or otherwise, often has its roots in feeling unappreciated.

I felt honored that Janette had the courage to share her pain with me. And I realized that the most powerful witness I could give would be to tell her what the Saviour had done for me. I knew that it wasn't the uniqueness of my tale that offered hope, but the very normalcy of my experience that makes it worth sharing. So I sat down to write my story.

~

Rows of light oak pews and mauve plush carpeting yawned between me and the gnarled little man behind the podium—a virtual chasm. I stared unseeing as he droned on about some remote mission station in Zambia, or was it a medical clinic in Bolivia? I don't remember. I leaned back and stared at the light fixtures. *Oh, God, I can't take much more of this.*

I tuned out the quivering notes of "In the Sweet By and By" and eyed the frozen chosen around me, ice carvings of the perfect Christian. "If someone fired a heat-seeking missile at this church, it would go straight through the walls and out the other side," I murmured under my breath, wrapping my arms securely about myself. A chill lingering between me and my siblings-in-Christ, brothers and sisters miles apart from one another, all wearing faces lifted from the pages of the book of Lamentations. *Is this all there is?* my heart cried.

"Having a form of godliness, but denying the power thereof." The words of 2 Timothy 3:5 accosted my mind, bouncing off the walls of my consciousness like a top spinning into its last frenzy before wobbling to a stop. I shook my head.

I didn't like the analogy. *Them, Lord, not me.* They *are the whited sepulchers.* But I knew better.

That day, as the morning sun spilled onto my gray wool suit skirt, I felt like an empty shell, a plastic, empty-headed Barbie doll lacking the advantages of to-die-for cheekbones and a micro-tiny waist. *I wonder if Mattel makes a chubby Barbie?* I laughed silently, a feeble attempt to ease the fear gnawing inside of me ". . . a form of godliness . . ."

My smile faded. *Have I come this far? Have I played by the rules of this game of Christianity for so long only to lose it all?* At that point it wouldn't have mattered if I called myself a Methodist, a Lutheran, or a Seventh-day Adventist. My church affiliation at that moment meant little if anything because, as one Christian evangelist put it: "If the bottle's empty, it doesn't matter what label is on it."

I mouthed the rest of the text. ". . . denying the power thereof." *Power? Power? Where is that power You promised?* I felt like I was slipping down a hole. I desperately looked around me for something, anything I could cling to before I disappeared into the blackness of my mind. *God, if Your power is real, if I really am Your daughter, if salvation is really mine, help me. Help me now. I don't want to lose it all.* I recalled a book I'd recently read: *Games Christians Play: An Irreverent Guide to Religion Without Tears.* In it authors Judi Culbertson and Patti Bard take a penetrating look at the church and at the games played each week by the members of the body of Christ. They call it a "beginner's handbook to Christian games, or how to live like the devil and still be a saint." ❋

Games in church? Oh, yes. The games began in Eden. There Adam played a church game called "If it weren't for you, I would . . ." He directed his game not only at his wife, Eve, but also at God. Christian husbands and wives have been playing that one ever since. Other games include Prima Donna, I'd Love to, but . . . , Have You Heard About Poor . . . , Why Don't They Do Something About . . . , I Don't Mean to Criticize, but . . . , My Bible's More Underlined Than Yours, and Busy Bee Me. And I'd played them all.

I stored these games in my spiritual toy box to pull out whenever my spirits sagged or wavered. And usually they worked for me, until that Sabbath morning when I came face-to-face with the truth. I needed something more than an elaborate entertainment center, more than an adrenaline rush or an emotional high. "I can't do it any longer, Lord. I feel like a live Raggedy Ann, trapped in a toy box of my own making."

I remembered how my toy box could become a boat, a car, a cave, a roller coaster—anything I wanted it to be. Sometimes, when my troubles seemed more than I could handle, I'd climb inside and shut the lid. There I'd hide until I became too cramped and I'd need to throw back the lid and escape.

"You know I love You, Father. You know the desire of my heart is to serve You. I can't just walk away. I don't want to lose You, but something's got to change. A form of godliness is no longer enough, Lord. I'm tired of playing church. I want to feel Your power within me."

What a revolution my prayer started that morning. It wouldn't be an easy journey. Like grapes off a cluster, God's truths would be hand-picked for me by the Holy Spirit, one at a time and at just the right time. I didn't realize I needed to come to this moment of spiritual stagnation before I was in a place where the Holy Spirit could move me. I didn't understand how my frenzy of good works had kept me from "seeing" the reality of God's love and experiencing His power in my life. And most of all, I couldn't comprehend the growing that would take place within me once I was ready to be real with God and myself.

---

*Judi Culbertson and Patti Bard, *Games Christians Play* (New York: Harper and Row, 1968), p. 7.

CHAPTER TWO

Playing Church

M y mother's eyes misted whenever she recalled the sermons I preached to my dolls and stuffed animals each week. Playing church at 5 years old was cute. However, playing church at 45 was pitiful. The adjustment that the Holy Spirit chose to make in my thinking was my penchant for playing at church.

"After all my years of faithful service, must I eat with swine before I can experience the joy the apostle Paul writes about? Must I eat the husks saved for pigs before I can enjoy my father's prime veal?" I cried aloud. "Sometimes I just want to be free!"

Clips from the story of the prodigal son flashed through my mind. I thought, *Kay, you are even more pitiful than he. At least he had a few months of partying and debauchery to enjoy before returning to the hayfields. His older brother was right! Why should his little brother have all the fun?*

I reviewed the dossiers of the three main characters in the story of Luke 15. A patient, and forgiving father, the epitome of love; an errant younger son who chafed under the restrictions of home; and the steady, hardworking, resentful older brother.

"You never fixed roast beef for me, Dad," the older brother accused. "I'm the one who's stayed faithfully by you. Where was my little brother when I bent my back in the hot sun, planting your corn, or when I arose before dawn to milk your cattle? Where was he when I mucked out the stalls and repaired the broken fences?"

I snapped alert. *The older sister? Is this a portrait of me?* The special musics I'd sung; the holiday programs I casted, directed, costumed, and produced; the camp meetings I'd attended; the potlucks when I stood with my hands deep in greasy dishwater while others gathered around a guest speaker, gleaning his knowledge; the phone calls I placed; the committees I'd chaired; the chocolate fudge nut cakes I *didn't* eat at potlucks to set the proper example! To what end? Another 30 or 40 years of similar service?

The truth was I couldn't take 30 more years. "Ye shall know the truth, and the truth shall make you free" (John 8:32). The truth was I couldn't take 30 more years of the same. Yet I didn't yearn to frolic through the minefields of sin. My all-too-practical mind realized that for every night of foolish pleasure a bitter, cold morning followed. No, my restlessness didn't come from a craving for exciting and forbidden pleasures.

I recognized my heavenly Father's goodness and His love. So many times I'd seen the hand of God turn potential tragedy into miraculous joy. How many auto accidents had I seen averted? Through health problems and family crises I'd been warmed and cosseted by divine love. Like the older brother in the story, I'd walked mile after mile by my Father's side, our voices lifted in praise. Yet suddenly I realized I never really knew Him.

The older brother's frustration burned inside of me. I envied the gleam in my younger brother's eyes whenever he waxed verbose about his debauched life and about the love he now had for our Father—his Saviour. I wanted to experience the high of redemption without wallowing in the pit of despair.

The simple message of "I have the joy, joy, joy, down in my heart" had long since faded, leaving a residue of disillusionment and apathy. The toddler who'd many years previously placed her flannel-backed heart as close to the picture of Jesus as possible had disappeared in a flurry of good works that defied logic.

Saints of biblical times didn't seem to ride the emotional and spiritual roller coasters I rode. They surrendered themselves to God and were instantly filled with freedom, joy, and peace. While I didn't doubt their experience, I wondered if they knew something I didn't.

I wondered if all that freeing and life-changing experience promised in God's Word was something meant for only the early Christians and the people of Hebrews 11. Lacking the peace I wanted, I substituted words like "worry" for the more Christlike "concern." I used "righteous indignation" in place of anger. And to replace the promised joy that was missing in my life, I sighed and accepted status quo as my "lot in life."

Maybe I'm expecting too much, I argued. After all, not everyone can sing like Sandi Patty or write like Madeleine L'Engle. And I certainly would never preach like Billy Graham! Perhaps the joy mentioned in Philippians was experienced only by super Christians, not for those of us confronting ragweed allergies, overextended credit cards, and approaching menopause.

But I decided I wouldn't give up without a fight. Like Jacob I would wrestle with God until He blessed me. When I mentioned this to a friend of mine, he said, "Did you know that wrestling is the only sport where one never loses contact with his opponent?" I liked that. One way or another, I was determined to break out of my self-styled, religious toy box and experience the freedom of John 8:32: "Ye shall know the truth, and the truth shall make you free."

CHAPTER THREE

No Toy Boxes
in Prison

Minutes before Pilate turned the Saviour over to the frenzied mob, he asked the Teacher, "What is truth?" Jesus never answered his question. He left the prelate to ponder the question in the darkest hours of the night that followed. Considering the events that followed, I imagine the question haunted Pilate for years to come.

So, what is truth? If I wanted to be set free—and Scripture says the truth is what does it—I needed to seek the answer to Pilate's question. Jesus said, "Ask, and it shall be given you; seek, and ye shall find" (Matthew 7:7). When I began to ask and seek, step by step God kept His word.

I can only share with you what God did for me, one woman's journey toward wholeness in Christ Jesus. I'd never suggest that the path on which He took me will be the same as the one He'll choose for my sister or my brother. While the problems we face might be similar, they're never the same. Jesus, the Way, doesn't change, but how He deals with us individually does. The loving Parent that He is, He does what is best for each of His children.

When Jesus commanded the rich young ruler to sell all he had to give to the poor, He was addressing this particular man's problem. While the ruler may have needed to deal with a lack of compassion, my sister's problem might be gossip, and mine might be unresolved anger or impure thoughts. Timing is important. What speaks to one person's heart at one point in time doesn't necessarily touch the next woman's experience at that same time.

Ever since I first learned to read, I read the Bible. In school I took Old Testament classes, New Testament classes, classes on doctrine, classes on the life of Christ, classes on analyzing biblical poetry and prophecy. Yet this time when I began to study God's Word, it was as if I'd never seen the verses before.

The Bible gives several examples of how God reaches out in love to His children—through a burning bush and a raven, a pillar of fire and a storm, and more. He gives each of us what *we* need. To the orphan, He's a father; to the lonely, a friend; to the widow or divorcee, a husband. He is a lover to the heartbroken, a shepherd to the lost, and a physician to the sick. And He's not just sitting in heaven waiting for us to reach out to Him. He's using all the resources at His hand to reach us.

Because of these differences in our experiences, Jesus warned, "Judge not, that ye be not judged" (Matthew 7:1). When we judge one another's Christian experience, we thwart the work of the Holy Spirit, a very dangerous position indeed. That morning when I sat in church passing judgment on my fellow worshipers, I prevented the Holy Spirit from touching me directly or reaching me through them. My jaundiced observations showed that I needed healing, perhaps more than they. I was heartsick. Only the Great Physician could heal my heartburn.

Noted psychologist Carl Jung (1875-1961) observed, "Among all my patients in the second half of life—this is to say, over 35—there has not been one whose problem in the last resort was not finding a religious outlook on life. It is safe to say that every one of them fell ill because he had lost what the living religions of every age had given to their followers, and none of them has been really healed who did not regain his religious outlook." *

My journey toward wholeness in Jesus, toward living the abundant life God intended, began with seals. That's right—seals. I've often claimed that if I'd been born an animal instead of a human, I'm sure I'd be a seal. Not only do I resemble one in physique, but my family says I act like one too. Seals like to play. Can you think of a grander life than spending your days sleeping in the sun, grazing on your favorite foods, and cavorting in the surf? Oh, I don't mind working—working hard, in fact—but only as long as I'm experiencing pleasure. When it ceases to be fun, my incentive to work vanishes.

On this particular day I wasn't in the mood for conversation. I sat down on a park bench to ponder the direction my thoughts had been taking. Obviously something in me had to change. But how? What?

God didn't send a bolt of "new light" to startle me out of my lethargy. Instead, God used three of His tried and proven methods: nature, a brother's testimony, and His Word. And for good measure He threw in a television commercial and a traditional old hymn.

Unaware that He'd already set the answer of my prayer in motion, I wrapped my arms tightly about myself and watched the younger seals splash in the water while the oldsters sunbathed on the rock. Their obvious joy for living reminded me of a television commercial produced by the DuPont Company. I smiled to myself. I knew without a doubt that a fellow Christian must have produced the ad.

The tape showed seals frolicking in the surf, whales leaping in the waves, birds soaring toward the heavens, and other fowl and sea creatures celebrating life. Accompanying their joyous play was a selection from Beethoven's Ninth Symphony: the melody of "Joyful, Joyful, We Adore Thee." The unrestrained display of praise and joy never failed to lift my spirits.

"All Thy works with joy surround Thee . . ." I thought about the deaf composer. I wondered what it was like for him to write the music he heard in his head but never got to hear performed. But then, perhaps he had heard a live angelic performance of the hymn of adoration and praise before the King of the universe! I picked up my Bible and opened it to John 10:10, the text the pastor had used for his sermon that morning. "I am come that they might have life, and that they might have it more abundantly."

More abundantly, I thought, feeling far older and more tired than my 40-plus years. I gazed out over the water watching the seals play "king on the rock." I laughed as one large bull seal tumbled into the water, surfaced, and came back for more. *That's life abundant*, I mused. *Imagine being so free, so filled with life!*

I felt like a young child with my nose pressed against a windowpane, watching a party on the other side of the glass. I wanted in, but I couldn't reach the doorknob, and no one was around to open the door for me.

If I had to choose a word to describe my life right then, the word would be "adequate." Adequate food, adequate clothing, adequate fuel for the family Isuzu. I'd had bad things happen—loss of parents, miscarriages, loss of jobs—but so did everyone else who lived long enough. Yes, my life was adequate. "Lord," I prayed, "adequate isn't sufficient anymore."

I remembered singing about the way being "long and weary," about "trials and temptations" everywhere, and "troubles and sorrows." Perhaps I had it all wrong. Perhaps adequate is the best it gets in this world, with only occasional bursts of joy. I studied the sea creatures for several minutes longer. Could the word "abundance" have lost something in the translation? When I returned home, I checked it out.

Several Greek terms translate into the English word "abundance." But the root word that interested me, a former English teacher, the most was the Greek term *hyperbole* meaning excellence, exceeding greatness, or beyond measure.

Hyperbole is a figure of speech, a word picture that means gross exaggeration, "a 10-foot-tall ice-cream cone." For example, a mother uses hyperbole when she says, "If I told you once, I told you a thousand times to clean your room!" The number was used not for accuracy, but for effect.

Jesus said, "I come to give you a hyperbolic life," a life filled beyond measure, and with excellence. I liked the idea of a 10-foot-tall ice-cream cone of living. Make mine chocolate almond delight! Nonfat and low-cal, of course.

To understand Jesus' statement better, I read the verses surrounding the text. Jesus was speaking to a group of people after He healed the sightless man at the Temple gate. The agitated Pharisees could find no fault with Jesus, so they threw the healed man out of the Temple. When the healed man recognized his Healer, he fell down and worshiped Him.

At this point in the story, Jesus compares the Pharisees to thieves who break into sheep pens to steal the sheep. He assured His listeners that while thieves (like these false teachers) come to rob, kill, and destroy, He, the Son of man, came to give life. By following Him, one can have life, and "have it more abundantly."

It was obvious that the life of which the Master spoke went far beyond the act of breathing or existing as a brain-dead creature on a life-support system. It's life capitalized! LIFE. Life filled with abundant energy and abundant vitality. It's living a life that goes far beyond excellence and greatness. It's living to the max!

Gross exaggeration!

I found the word "abundant" used several times in both the Old and New Testaments of the Bible. In the Creation story, to describe the quantity of sea creatures God made. To describe the amount of water that flooded the earth and the number of frogs that invaded Egypt. New Testament writers used the word to describe the amount of wealth available to God's children in the Father's kingdom, and in such phrases as "out of the abundance of the heart," the mouth speaks (Luke 6:45). Jesus spoke of a multitude of angels being sent to earth when I am sure that a single one would do nicely. Throughout the entire Scriptures God proves Himself to be an abundant provider, a ruler who operates in an arena far bigger, wider, deeper, and higher than anything I could imagine.

In my mind the text that logically followed John 10:10 was "No eye has seen, no ear has heard, no mind has conceived what God has prepared for those who love him" (1 Corinthians 2:9, 10, NIV). Sounds like abundance to me. But I'd always thought of the text in terms of eternity, the reward awaiting the faithful when they got to heaven. I'd never before linked it with the promise Jesus gave for the rewards I could be enjoying right here on earth.

"But seek first his kingdom and his righteousness, and all these things will be given to you as well" (Matthew 6:33, NIV).

"OK, Lord," I begged, "teach me everything You can about Your kingdom." But before He answered my request, I received a phone call from one of my book editors asking me to write the story of Noble Alexander. Pastor Alexander was a lay preacher who'd been incarcerated in a Cuban prison for 22 years for preaching the gospel of Jesus Christ.

Instantly I thought, *No way. I can't do it.* I preferred to write light, happy stories, not depressing, oppressive tales of brutality and pain. And for good reason. Before I write, I must "live" my subject's experience. Quite frankly, I didn't look forward to "living" Pastor Alexander's story.

The thought of being imprisoned in a cement block cell for two days, let alone 22 years, sent me into the sweats. I remembered going to the city jail with our church youth group to sing to the prisoners. I can still feel the creepy crawlies running up and down my neck when I heard the iron-barred gates clang closed behind me.

I begged off, but my editor finally convinced me to talk with Pastor Alexander before saying no. Reluctantly I agreed. I fought against placing the promised phone call throughout the rest of the day. That night I gritted my teeth and punched the 11-digit number into my phone and waited, counting the rings. *One, two, three, maybe he's not home—too bad—four, five . . . Oh, well, I tried.* On the fifth ring I heard a click, and a male voice with a strong Caribbean accent said, "Hello?"

When I introduced myself, he recognized the name. My editor had prepared him for my call. He gave me a synopsis of his story, much like my editor had given me earlier in the day. But something was different when Pastor Alexander told it. Through 3,000 miles of telephone wire—or more precisely, through the sound waves that leap from the earth to a communication satellite in space and back again—I could hear an incredible sound in the man's voice. *Joy!* I shook my head in amazement. The joy bells were unmistakable, as clear as the myriad of church bells one hears while standing in the Boston Commons at high noon.

I listened in disbelief. I could detect no bitterness, no anger, and no signs of depression in his voice. The man deserved to have his name added to the eleventh chapter of Hebrews. By the time I hung up, I knew I'd write his story, if only to discover his source of joy.

Noble Alexander didn't set out to be a hero. His ordeal began one night after a youth revival meeting at the church that he pastored. What started as a five-minute police interrogation ended 22 long years later, thanks only to the intercession of an American politician negotiating with Castro for the release of American prisoners.

The news articles and Pastor Alexander's finely penned notes began to arrive in the mail. I couldn't believe the extent of the man's endurance. That one man could survive such atrocities and retain his sanity was remarkable in itself. Had I been the one imprisoned under those conditions, I'm afraid that within the first hour I'd have curled into a fetal position and prayed to die.

Lying on my waterbed in the comfort of my California home, I imagined each horror Noble described: the poisonous snakes and cockroaches, the rats, the tortures, the cramped conditions in filthy cells, the stench of human excrement. Many times my mind shut down for repairs. Even with my overactive imagination I couldn't come close to visualizing his ordeal. Yet, word by word, I recorded his story.

Beaten and left for dead; shrapnel permanently embedded in his body; teeth knocked down his throat; caged over rotting garbage; stripped of his clothes, his name, and all human dignity—it was an inventory of cruelty. I couldn't imagine how he survived being stuffed in a coffin-sized box with six other men for weeks at a time; how he maintained his sanity when subjected to Oriental water torture; how he kept from drowning when his captors submerged him in icy waters until he lost consciousness. Yet through everything he could still feel joy. I had dozens of questions that needed answering. How had he maintained his sanity? Was he such a macho human that he stood alone like an oak in a pasture during an ice storm? Did God reinforce his resiliency with heavenly steel?

I found it remarkable how the "pastor," as Noble was called by his fellow prisoners, spent his time between tortures. He didn't lie about his cell weeping and lamenting his fate, or whining over his lot in life. Instead, he went about the prison, relieving the suffering of the sick, sharing his food rations with the elderly, praying with the discouraged and dying—being a pastor.

From Castro's kingdom of terror this man of God preached of the abundance of the kingdom of love. While eating corn mush and mealworms, he reminded his fellow prisoners that God's kingdom was not about food and drink.

Facing unrelenting persecution from the Communist machine, Noble found other Christians. They banded together for strength, like trees supporting one another in a storm. Even the weakest sapling gains strength when supported by others. They established an underground church, not with First Baptist, Presbyterian, or Seventh-day Adventist emblazoned on the weekly bulletin, but with *agape* engraved on their hearts. Labels didn't matter when one's survival was in question.

The incarcerated family of God elected a church board and organized a choir. Imagine, a choir behind bars praising the God of liberty and freedom! Like Paul and Silas, the prison cell became a concert hall, attracting others to the Saviour.

The prisoners' greatest treasure was the Bible, or whatever portions they might have at any one time. When they had no Bible, they penned out the precious promises of

God's Word with a discarded building nail and their own blood for ink. They vowed, "We were born free; Christ set us free; and we will die free."

Not all the men who professed Christ's name survived. But those who did, like Pastor Alexander, found a freedom Fidel Castro couldn't grant, nor probably ever experience.

Free while in chains; free while staring at gray concrete block walls; free despite the eyes of their captors following their every move? *Surely their religion was more than an emotional roller coaster ride,* I decided. *Great on the hilltops and nonexistent when they hit the pits.*

I could see that these men had no time for religious games. They weren't "playing church" at La Cabana Prison. While they had little in the way of personal possessions, they were incredibly rich spiritually. Their faith stopped bullets. Their love for one another overrode Communist memorandums. Their joy defied the demons of suicide. While their bodies might be held captive in one of the most inhumane and brutal prison systems in the entire world, their spirits could not be broken.

"That's what I want, Lord." Remembering Paul's wry comment before King Agrippa, I hesitated. "Except for the prison cell, of course."

---

* In Kenneth L. Bakken and Kathleen H. Hoffeller, *The Journey Toward Wholeness: A Christ-centered Approach to Health and Healing* (New York: Crossroads, 1988), p. 40.

CHAPTER FOUR

Lifting the Lid

Many are asking, 'Who can show us any good?'" (Psalm 4:6, NIV). For me, Pastor Alexander's life answered the question asked in that text. He demonstrated "good" while enduring the most degrading conditions. *Surely,* I thought as I typed his story into my computer, *this man has suffered enough. Certainly he is worthy and ready to receive the kingdom of God.*

Jesus said, "Seek ye first the kingdom of God, . . . and all these things shall be added unto you" (Matthew 6:33). My emphasis always seemed to be more on how to acquire "all these things" than on the discovery of the kingdom of God. Pastor Alexander had the kingdom of God, but obviously not "all these things" if those "things" included the amenities we consider necessary like deodorant, shampoo, and a matching sofa and love seat.

However, the things Pastor Noble did have included love in the face of hate, peace instead of turmoil, and joy before understanding through endless pain. The "all these things" to which Jesus referred was obviously more than an afterthought at the end of the verse. It's as if Jesus was saying, "Oh yes, and all this stuff will be thrown in the deal."

I love to talk about heaven and the new earth. I love to sing, to read, and to dream about a city in which justice and truth will reign, sin will be no more, and peace will be a way of life. I believe it's important to do so, to keep the world to come real before our eyes. But what about the kingdom of God we can have *now*, right here in our hearts?

After Eve and Adam sinned, God did not leave them alone to sort things out by themselves. And He doesn't abandon us in spiritual and intellectual darkness today, to embrace every new fad, crackpot idea, or devil's deception. Jesus promised a life abundant. He said, "The truth shall make you free."

Two thousand years ago Christ came to a frightening planet filled with brutality and danger, on which human life was cheap. Oppressed by a foreign dictator, Jewish leaders and peasants alike looked to the coming Messiah as a savior, not from their sins, but an escape from their burdensome world. Pregnant mothers prayed that their unborn sons would be the "promised one," the one who would rally the bands of rogue dissidents into an army. The young and not so young lions of Judah preached of the arrival of a military general who would end Rome's hated occupation of their country.

So when Jesus spoke about His coming kingdom, people listened. This Man could feed the hungry bellies of their soldiers by the flick of His wrist. With a touch He could restore limbs slashed off in battle, and breathe life back into the bodies of men killed by the enemy. And best of all, He could fulfill their wildest dream—to crush the Roman army back to the marble staircase of Caesar's palace.

The crowd leaned forward to catch the Teacher's every word. Oh yes, He had their attention. But what He said baffled them. He drew a child to His side and said, "I tell you the truth, unless you change and become like little children, you will never enter the kingdom of heaven" (Matthew 18:3, NIV).

Like a child? How can this be? they wondered. Surely to win the Jewish-occupied territory from Rome, Christ would need strong fearless warriors, not little children!

In the harsh world of the first century, children died by the dozens from disease and disasters. Their value was insignificant until they matured enough to earn their own way by working in the fields and home.

World conditions and attitudes haven't improved much since then. Children are still considered dispensable by much of society. Three million alone die each year from poverty-related illnesses. I weep for the innocent bystander killed from bullets being exchanged by rival gangs, and I long to escape this world for a better land. But are my tears any different from those of Galilee peasant women, praying for a redeemer? Who wouldn't want to escape from this world to a better place?

Politicians spend millions seeking solutions to the problem of violence in the streets, to malnutrition, to homelessness, to communicable diseases as diverse as AIDS and the common cold. But rather than finding solutions, they uncover a nest of problems previously not considered. Over the years legislators have passed laws and proposed plans to create what they hoped would be better kingdoms.

Despite these laws and plans, many of us still live as prisoners in our homes—if we have homes. Every day thousands of young girls and boys numb their reality with drugs and alcohol. Old people are warehoused instead of revered. For all the plans—and hopes and dreams—we've had for a better tomorrow, we still breathe air laced with auto fumes; we drink water filtered through contaminated soil; and we eat foods enriched with lethal sprays.

Naturally the idea of a paradise in which peace, joy, and love rule attracts Christians and non-Christians alike. Anything to escape the reality of our day-by-day existence.

What is your idea of paradise? If money were not an issue, what kind of kingdom would you construct? A Disneyland playground? A luxurious castle with a retinue of hovering servants? A Fantasy Island where your every whim is magically granted?

What is your enchanted land? To the prisoner in chains, heaven is a soaring eagle. To the prostitute, it is the restoration of one's virginity and the gift of being able to trust again. To the lupus patient, paradise means no more pain. To newlyweds, it's a vine-covered cottage or a tax-free condo in the Bahamas. To the aging grandmother, it is the fountain of eternal youth.

Walt Disney used his genius to create the Magic Kingdom, a place that incorporated all the elements of man's ideas for a perfect world. He built a place that would always be clean and orderly; a place where children could run about freely and safely; a place where people could—for a few hours—forget their troubles and fears, where they could laugh and become as little children once more. But when day is over we dreamers must reclaim our baggage of worry or pain or loneliness and trudge home to our own stark reality. Even the genius of Walt Disney cannot truly override reality.

Then what is the kingdom of God? Though many of us are fuzzy on what it actually is—fluffy clouds and angels; a world of youth, security, and order; a fantasy island in the sun—we still want to go there. A recent poll revealed that 95 percent of all Americans believe they will go to heaven, wherever heaven is. But they aren't so sure about their nearest neighbors and their coworkers.

The phrase "kingdom of God" comes from the Greek abstract verb *basileia,* meaning sphere of God's rule, a place where His sovereignty is acknowledged, where people submit to His rule. Biblical references to the kingdom of God fall into two classes: the future as a material and physical reward for the faithful; and the present, a spiritual and moral state of being.

I could handle the concept of the future reward as referred to in 2 Thessalonians 1:5. I'd been taught from infancy that if I'm good, I'd go to heaven. My problem has always been the "being good" part. That's what caused my frustration in the first place. The real flesh-and-blood Kay could never measure up to the perfect celluloid Kay I envisioned.

My only hope rested in discovering the truth about the other kingdom of God, the present tense kingdom mentioned in Luke 17:21. "The kingdom of God is in the midst of you" (RSV).

Right here? Right now? In the flesh? I eyed the oatmeal

cookie I held in my hand. *It's the flesh that causes me so many of my problems.* But, the Word reminded, "the kingdom of God is not food and drink, but righteousness and peace and joy in the Holy Spirit" (Romans 14:17, NKJV). I could see how the future kingdom of flesh could change my life, but wondered how a Spirit kingdom could rule over my "fleshy" one in the here and now?

First Corinthians 4:20 told me that the kingdom of God is not a matter of talking, but of power. I could use a little power in my life. *Yes,* I thought. *This is for me, Lord. This is my kind of place.* Like the future kingdom, the present kingdom of God could not be inherited through my mama's or daddy's assets, but only through the Spirit's control (1 Corinthians 15:50). And "no one can see the kingdom of God unless he is born again" (John 3:3, NIV). I recalled the story of Christ's midnight visitor.

Nicodemus listened from afar to Jesus' stories about the kingdom of God, and he hungered for more. But the young Pharisee waited for the crowds to go home to their own villages before approaching the Man people called the "Messiah." As Jesus and His followers settled down for the night, Nicodemus slipped into the camp and found Jesus.

Knowing the man's desire for secrecy, the Master didn't invite him into the friendly circle of disciples. Instead He allowed him to draw Him out into the protective darkness of night. Once there, Jesus waited for him to speak.

"Rabbi, we know You're a teacher sent from God," Nicodemus began. "For no one can perform the miraculous signs You are doing if God were not with Him."

We? At the man's less than personal claim, I can imagine the Saviour lifting an eyebrow, a grin tweaking one corner of His mouth. He recognized the "distance" Nicodemus desired to put between his heart and the Saviour. Like a waiter in a swanky restaurant who haughtily uses the pronoun "we" instead of "I," the Jewish scholar hesitated to reveal more than a passing professional interest in Jesus.

In reply, Jesus took the analogy of becoming as a child

two steps further, past infancy directly to the unborn baby. "I tell you the truth, no one can enter the kingdom of God unless he is born again" (John 3:3, NIV).

"Born again?" Nicodemus's voice was puzzled, his face hidden by the shadows of night. "Born again? Must I return to my mother's womb?" he asked, partly in jest.

Jesus ignored the man's wit and honed in on his heart. "I tell you the truth, no one can enter the kingdom of God unless he is born of water and the Spirit. Flesh gives birth to flesh, but the Spirit gives birth to spirit" (John 3:5, 6, NIV).

As the Master continued speaking, the jaded Pharisee knew that he wanted what Jesus offered. But his intellect argued, *Could it be so easy?* Nicodemus had been born and raised in a legalistic society. He'd always played by the rules. He worked hard at serving God. But as a result, he had serious problems with guilt and a sense of failure. In his mind he could never measure up to the man he wanted to be. He lived under condemnation of the law.

But at that point in his life Nicodemus could have listened to Christ talk until the dawn broke over the distant Judean hills and not understood a word. He could not understand until Jesus opened his mind. And through that understanding, the teacher of Jewish theology would be reborn of the Spirit.

Born again. In recent years the expression "born again" has been bantered about so freely that it's become little more than a cliché, an ID tag in the Christian subculture. I, too, claimed to be born again . . . and again . . . and again. I knew that my sins had been forgiven and that my conversions were prompted by the Holy Spirit. What I wanted to know was why I couldn't keep the spiritual and emotional high that was supposed to accompany my new birth. What life-sustaining ingredient was missing from my recipe for abundant Christian living?

Wait! Hold it! Today's headlines should read "Satan Is a Liar!" This world of scarcity isn't all there is. For being born again entitles me to the reality of God's kingdom. And it can be mine—today, now!

When Jesus sent His disciples out to preach the message that the kingdom of God had come, they themselves didn't understand what their Lord was saying. He wasn't speaking in the physical as they thought, or in the abstract of an unseen future. He meant that "the kingdom of God" was at hand then, and He means it is at hand now. But this obvious truth came to me in a roundabout way.

Seated again on a park bench by the bay, I watched a lone seal in the water, grazing for its supper. First it'd float facedown, then it'd arch its back and disappear into the icy Pacific waters. Several seconds later it'd surface with a shellfish in its mouth. I could hear the shells crack between the seal's jaws as it ate its catch. After finishing each course, the seal rolled onto its back and clapped its flippers as if thanking God for its supper.

The seal's behavior ignited my playful nature. I envisioned the Creator sitting on a royal blue velvet-cushioned throne, smiling down on the seal, perhaps chuckling aloud. *I* laughed out loud at the idea. But then the more reasonable, intellectual side of me replaced my flippant flight of fantasy.

The logical Kay—the Kay who scolds me when I spill a dollop of soup on my blouse or berates me further if the blouse is new or I'm attending a special event—argued with my playful nature. *Stop trying to personify a dumb animal. The seal's merely cleaning the crumbs off its flippers,* the bossy Kay said. But as quickly as the splash of reality hit, the words of Psalm 148 entered my mind: "Praise the Lord from the earth, you great sea creatures and all ocean depths" (verse 7, NIV).

H'mm, wait a minute, I thought. *If David the king could write about the sea creatures praising God, my thoughts can't be that far removed from reality. What does the seal know that I don't?* While my flippered friend might dine alfresco, its life is far from a picnic. It has to battle the barnacles of life too. It deals with the sharks as well as the humans that threaten its daily survival. Yet, according to the psalmist the seal praises God.

I opened my Bible to read the entire one hundred forty-eighth psalm. I found that the fruit trees and the mountains;

the hills, the waters, and the shining stars; the wild animals and cattle; the small creatures and flying birds were created to praise the Lord.

Psalm 66 takes the visual one step further. "All the earth bows down to you; . . . they sing praise to your name" (verse 4, NIV). My spirits soared as I read several more praise psalms. My interest had been teased. I wanted to learn more about this "praise" business.

I looked up the word "praise" in my computer Bible concordance and found more than 300 invitations to praise God. Imagine! More than 300! I found most of them in the poetry of David. King David—a murderer, a schemer, an adulterer—but a man singled out as being "a man after God's own heart" because he truly repented and followed God with his whole heart.

In the thirtieth psalm he wrote, "You turned my wailing into dancing. . . . O Lord my God, I will give you thanks forever" (verses 11, 12, NIV). Dancing! I laughed at my two left feet. *That's what I need, a little spirit-filled dancing in my life.*

The prophet Isaiah described the trees as "clapping their hands for joy" (see Isaiah 55:12). I could visualize that. During a High Sierra autumn the golden leaves of the aspens flutter in the sunlight like the hands of an appreciative audience applauding a musical performance.

And talk about praise services! When Jesus rode into Jerusalem on the Sunday before His death, the people shouted their praises to Him. Those whose tongues He'd loosened shouted the loudest. Those who'd once been without sight led the procession. Cripples leaped for joy, and healed lepers spread their coats on the ground before Him. Lazarus, brought back to life from the dead, led the donkey on which the Master rode. The joy of the people was spread all the way to Jerusalem and into the solemn halls of the Sanhedrin.

Worried about the Roman guard's reaction, the Pharisees sent an entourage to quiet the mob. They had reasons to be concerned. If the Romans mistook the people's celebration for an insurrection, the entire Jewish community would suffer. But when the Pharisees begged Jesus to quiet the mob, He replied, "If these people hold their peace, the stones will cry out."

Stones? Inanimate stones praising God? That isn't so outlandish. There is an island off the coast of Scotland called the Isle of Eigg, where it is reported that the sands sing. Responding to the amount of pressure, the temperature, the moisture in the air, and other atmospheric conditions, the minuscule quartz crystals emit musical tones, from highest soprano to lowest bass. Walk across the sand, filter it through your fingers, toss a handful into the air, and it produces music—songs of praise. Theoretically we could conduct an entire symphony out there on the beach. Fires the imagination, doesn't it?

I thought about the phenomenon of Eigg and, like a tiny spark from a match being struck against granite, a chorus of praise glimmered inside me. I'd sung the words to the little chorus "I Love You, Lord" dozens of times but never "heard" the words, especially about my voice sounding pleasant unto God. Most of the sounds coming from my mouth over the past few years had been anything but sweet. I'd emitted a litany of gripes, complaints, and whinery. The lyrics to my "songs" had been filled with sarcasm, criticism, with self-pity. Tears welled up in my eyes. I'd been challenging God to prove Himself to be the Father of joy, the God of peace, and He used a simple sea creature to challenge me to praise Him.

The trees, the surf, the sand, the skies, the squabbling gulls—all around me I began to see signs of His love and care. All around me His creation praised Him for His goodness. I was the one out of line. I was the one not listening. *How sad*, I thought, *that man or (in my case) woman, the crown of His creation, is the only element of His creation that must be prompted to praise Him.* Suddenly I had an insatiable appetite to learn more about this thing called praise.

I discovered that praise acknowledges God's supremacy. He is worthy of our praise not only for what He's done but for who He is. *Yadah*, the Hebrew word for praise, means to confess, to shout jubilation, to give thanks. A more literal interpretation of the term would be "Let us praise Yah, Yahweh, or He who causes to be [the Creator]." Any wonder why all nature praises? The term *yadah* overlaps in meaning with a number of other Hebrew words for praise, such as *hallel*, from which we get hallelujah. It's interesting to note that the equivalent of the word hallelujah is found in every spoken language.*

Praise puts our lives into a proper perspective with God. Our unworthiness glares at us in flashing neon lights when we measure our goodness up to God's. This, in turn, leads us to confession, or—that's right—praise. From here, confession and the subsequent forgiveness circles us once again to praise and thanksgiving for what He's done. Loops of praise, circles of praise within circles of praise. *Could this be, I wondered, the secret Paul wrote about in Philippians 4:4, "Rejoice in the Lord always"?*

The second Hebrew verb for "praise," *hallel*, is my favorite. *Hallel* is the intensive form of the verb meaning "to boast." I like the idea of boasting of God's love. We boast of our accomplishments, of our possessions, of our children's accomplishments, why not of God, the one responsible for everything?

Used for the first time in Genesis by the princes of Pharaoh to praise Sarah's beauty to Pharaoh, *hallel* also means to celebrate, to sing, and to glorify. The word *hallel*, loosely translated, means "praise the Lord." While the entire book of Psalms is considered the book of praise or *hallel*, Jewish scholars single out Psalms 113-118 as the *hallel* psalms. These songs were sung each year at Passover time. Jesus sang the *hallel* psalms in the upper room the night before His death. Even as He sang the songs of celebration and joy with His friends, He knew that within a few short hours He'd be agonizing alone in Gethsemane.

I never picture that fateful night to be one of celebration. Shadows haunt the corners of the room. The faces of the disciples are drawn and solemn. Jesus' face is lined with grief.

If I were an artist, I think I would try to capture the mood of the group before Judas's treachery was revealed. If I were a portrait painter, I would attempt to reproduce the glowing face of Jesus as He sang to His Father, "Praise the Lord. . . . Let the name of the Lord be praised, both now and forevermore. From the rising of the sun to the place where it sets, the name of the Lord is to be praised" (Psalm 113:1-3, NIV). "I love the Lord, for he heard my voice" (Psalm 116:1, NIV). "This is the day the Lord has made; let us rejoice and be glad in it. . . . Give thanks to the Lord, for he is good; his love endures forever" (Psalm 118:24-29, NIV).

The Scriptures tell us that praise builds strength: "The joy of the Lord is my strength" (Nehemiah 8:10, NIV). I wonder how much strength the *hallel* praises gave the Saviour during the torturous hours that followed.

---

*W. E. Vine, Merrill F. Unger, William White, Jr., editors, *Vine's Expository Dictionary of Biblical Words* (Nashville: Thomas Nelson Publishers, 1985), pp. 184, 195.

CHAPTER FIVE

A New Song

My search for information on praise led me to the word "rejoice," the New Testament equivalent to praise. "Rejoice in the Lord, always," I read, and "In every thing give thanks" (Philippians 4:4, NIV; 1 Thessalonians 5:18).

Rejoice always? Give thanks in everything, I thought as I tightened the laces of my walking shoes. *Just how literal does Paul mean for me to take this?* Determined, I stepped out into the night air and took a deep breath. "OK, God. Remember this is Your idea not mine. But if You say to do it, I'll obey."

I strode across the neighboring school's empty playing field, my arms swinging and my back straight, singing in full voice, "Hallelu, hallelujah, praise ye the Lord . . ." By the second lap, I felt pretty good. I switched to another praise chorus. *H'mm, maybe there's something to this praise stuff after all.* By the third lap I decided to try the giving thanks part. After I exhausted the typical words of gratitude for my cozy home and family, I searched for more creative things about which to thank Him. "All things, eh? In this command, Lord, do You include such things in life as my asthma?"

My life had been miserable since I'd developed chronic asthma while living among the eucalyptus trees in Oregon. I hated the weakness that prevented me—on frequent writing-related trips—from walking comfortably from my car to the airport terminal without stopping several times to rest. I detested waking in the night gasping for my next breath. I loathed the incontinence that accompanied the worst of the attacks. At one point my doctor told me I'd never sing again. But at least I could sing, after a fashion.

"OK, here goes!" I'd start *praising* God. Without breaking stride, I chanted, "I rejoice, O God, for my asthma. Thank You for reminding me that You are the sustainer of life. Thank You for breathing life into woman and she became a living soul." I prayed this prayer of praise lap after lap until my chanting turned to singing. By the time I returned to my house, I coughed from the exertion, but I felt the joy of victory. My Nikes and I had completed the first stage of God's retraining program for me. The irony that the Greek word *nike* means victory didn't escape me either.

I didn't know until much later that I'd stumbled upon an important praise key that night. Praise is a *choice*, not a response. I make an intellectual choice to praise, not because I feel exhilarated and alive, but because God asked me to praise. It is evidence of my allegiance to Him.

In the Scriptures the words "praise" and "thanksgiving" are often used interchangeably. However, whenever the Bible writers use both terms in the same verse there is a subtle difference between the two. Perhaps you're thinking, *You're splitting hairs, Kay. Who cares if you say "thank you" or "praise God," as long as you acknowledge Him?*

But wait. The expression "thank you" is used as a response to a kindness. Saints, sinners, and cynics alike say thank you for services rendered. That's gratitude, and just good manners.

For example, when my husband hauls the garbage can to the curb on Thursday morning for pickup or when he remembers to refuel my Isuzu for me, I respond by saying thank you. I appreciate having the garbage emptied and my car ready to roll. That's thanksgiving.

But when he's standing at the kitchen sink getting a drink of water, and I come up behind him, wrap my arms around his waist, and growl in his ear, "What a lion of a man I married—I love you so much," that's praise. Not for what he has done for me, but for who and what kind of person he is. The thanks for the refueled car is appreciated, but my "just because" praise puts a twinkle in his eyes.

Everyone appreciates praise, from the tiniest child to the eldest grandpa. God isn't so different. Considering the history of His people since Creation, I'm sure He appreciates our every word and thought of gratitude. The entire Old Testament is a canon of ingratitude. God brought water from the rock to quench His people's thirst in the wilderness, and they griped. He fed them manna from His own table, and they whined for the leeks and garlics and flesh pots of Egypt. He rarely heard a thank You from the Israelites. Certainly He is pleased when we thank Him for the blessings with which He fills our lives.

However, gratitude alone focuses still on ourselves, on "what you do for me or I can do for you, or what God does for me." On the other hand, praise takes our minds off ourselves and our situation in life, and focuses our attention on our Creator. As Don Matzat, the author of *Truly Transformed*, writes: "Prayer and praise changes our hearts and directs our minds to God so that we might receive Him."[1]

I liked that. I needed a redirection of my mind toward God. I spent too much time focusing on me and my problems. I needed to learn how to pray in the Spirit of abundance and praise.

Jesus began the Lord's Prayer with praise. "Our Father which art in heaven, hallowed be thy name. Thy kingdom come. Thy will be done in earth, as it is in heaven" (Matthew 6:9, 10). When we cry, "King of kings and Lord of lords," we praise. When we sing, ". . . worship His majesty," we praise. The prayer He prayed at the Passover feast for His disciples also began with praise.

Twenty-four hours a day angels bow before the throne of God in praise. Heaven has no more treasured assignment for an angel than this one. And when we praise, our praise joins theirs. What an honor to be included in such elite society! Since discovering this attitude of praise, I've wondered many times if Lucifer's first sin wasn't committed the moment he chose to stop praising God. I wondered if he fell long before he grumbled his first gripe or mumbled his first complaint against the Father? Could his discontent and envy have been the result of ceasing to praise? Which came first?

And now, millenniums later, our praises continually remind Satan of all he's lost. I suspect the reason Lucifer works so hard to keep the truth of this from humans is that he knows that this is a privilege he lost and can never regain. And he knows firsthand that praising God brings us strength (see Nehemiah 8:10). It makes sense that the first thing he'd want to destroy in the face of trouble would be our joy. After we lose our joy, our defenses topple like dominoes lined up on a card table.

Some critics argue that praise is a lightweight doctrine compared to the weightier matters of the law. These same people often class the command to "love one another" in the same category. However, both concepts are the very taproots of the gospel, without which our worship would be in vain. Love and praise are the essence of who we are as God's adopted children. The controversy of the ages rests on whether or not God truly loves us, and whether we can trust that love. Our praise acknowledges He is God.

Satan accused God of being unloving and unreliable, and he uses the same tactics on you and me. He plants niggling doubts in our minds so that we will question God's love for us. But each time we speak His praises and live out His love, we demonstrate the attitude of Christ living in us and we declare our allegiance to Him.

Ephesians 1:3-5 tells us that God's children were predestined to praise Him. In 1 Peter 2:9 Peter says that "you are a chosen people, a royal priesthood, a holy nation, a people belonging to God" (NIV). When the apostle spoke of the chosen, he used the Greek word *eklektos*, from which we get the word "elect." We were elected to serve God. *Eklektos* is also used in Revelation 17:14 for "chosen and faithful followers" (NIV).

Why have we been chosen? The verse reveals the unique feature that delineates us as people belonging to God: "That you may declare the praises of him who called you out of darkness into his wonderful light" (NIV).

Our reason for being! I was created for the express purpose of praising God. I'd read these verses hundreds of times. I'd heard them quoted in sermons, but somehow I totally missed the application. My reason for being is to shout to the world, "Praise God for His incredible goodness. He is so great!" But as He did with the disciples in Luke 24:37, Jesus needed to open my eyes supernaturally to the truth of my position.

I've discovered that praising God is great when I feel like it. With my sanguine personality I can hyperventilate praising God on sunny days. And central California has an incredible number of sunny days. But what about the times when I don't feel like praising Him?

Face it, the world's a pretty grim place. And life is seldom fair. Is this business of praising more than the same old toy box religion I'd been playing for years? Would living in the rain forest of Oregon, or perched on a rocky crag along the brooding coastline of Maine alter my enthusiastic praise? It might, if praise was meant to be the result of enthusiasm instead of my conscious choice.

Thirty some years ago I chose to love my husband, for better or worse. I chose to love him on his good days and on his bad. I chose to love him on *my* good and bad days as well. There are times I might not like him very much, but I still love him — that is a choice I make. I am grateful that Richard makes my choice easy to keep.

Praising God is similar. I choose to praise God despite my circumstances. This greater gift is what the author of Hebrews called the sacrifice of praise. The sacrifice of praise is the "fruit of lips that confess his name" (Hebrews 13:15, NIV).

Again and again the psalmist gave us examples of bringing to God our sacrifice of praise. Sometimes in the beginning of a poem David implored God to grind the bones of his enemies into dust, but by the end of the poem—his prayer—he was praising God for His goodness. However, my favorite biblical example of the sacrifice of praise is found in the book of Habakkuk:

> "Though the fig tree does not bud
> and there are no grapes on the vines,
> though the olive crop fails
> and the fields produce no food,
> though there are no sheep in the pen
> and no cattle in the stalls,
> yet I will rejoice in the Lord,
> I will be joyful in God my Savior"
> (Habakkuk 3:17, 18, NIV).

As with the Old Testament prophet, how much more God appreciates my praise on days when I don't feel like it—when the car breaks down alongside a busy highway during a cloudburst, when my husband learns I accidentally overdrew the family bank account, or my daughter comes home from school and announces she's been exposed to measles.

God felt the chilling rains that turned the dusty paths of Galilee into mud. He knew about creative financing when He sent Peter fishing for tax tribute. God understood the anxiety that accompanies pain and death. He said, "Let your conversation be without covetousness" (Hebrews 13:5) and "Be content with what you have, because God has said, 'Never will I leave you; never will I forsake you'" (verse 5, NIV). That covers everything. Whatever our circumstances might be, He's promised to be with us. As Pastor Noble Alexander stood chin-deep in a Cuban prison's cesspool for obeying God rather than his Communist captors, he could know he was not alone. God had promised to be with him. And He was.

Christians trapped in war zones can know for certain they're not alone. God said, "Never will I leave you; never will I forsake you." That's never! If this were the only promise our Father in heaven made and kept, He would be worthy of our continued praise.

I love to sing—new songs, old songs, silly songs, high- and lowbrow songs, even the ditties on TV commercials. Friends and family know that I am likely to burst into song at any time and any place. I've been overheard singing to myself while grocery shopping, while waiting in line at the DMV, and while crossing hotel parking lots. On one all-night road trip from San Diego to Albuquerque, to keep Richard awake while driving, I sang my way through the old *Singing Youth* book.

When our daughters developed into "touch-me-not" travelers, I soothed frayed nerves by singing. That's how Rhonda and Kelli learned to harmonize—riding in the car. Over the years our family has endured thousands of miles and hundreds of verses of "Hey Lidy," "Three Wheels on My Wagon," and "You Are My Sunshine." As a result (at least I would like to think it's because of and not in spite of), both daughters are professional musicians.

But after I got asthma, I couldn't sing. Even one note sent me into spasms of coughing. When I asked my respiratory specialist how long it would be before my voice returned, he shook his head. "Chances are you'll never be able to sing again with any volume. Once the lungs have been injured as badly as yours are, there will always be scars."

Devastated, I stumbled from the medical building to my car and sobbed into my steering wheel for 15 minutes. Singing had been my life since as a 5-year-old I first stood in front of church and belted out a dramatic rendition of "Are You Ready for Jesus to Come?"

For 13 months the doctor's prophecy proved correct. His words might still be true today except I took my problem to a wiser Physician. "He put a new song in my mouth, a hymn of praise to our God" (Psalm 40:3, NIV).

My singing voice returned slowly. I'd been praying for months that God would do something about my chronic illness. More and more the disease inhibited my speaking ministry. I would return from a speaking engagement exhausted, not from the rigors of travel, but from the new antigens that triggered a fresh round of allergies that aggravated my lung condition. And I knew that the medicine I required was actually damaging my body even as it eased my breathing.

I began praying for divine healing. I reasoned that if my God is the same today as He was when He walked beside the Sea of Galilee, when He breathed life into a little girl's nostrils, and when He re-created eyeballs out of mud and spit for Bartimaeus — this same Jesus could heal my battered, scarred lungs. At least it was worth my study and my prayer time.

I began praying in the traditional manner. That is, begging and pleading with God as if I could play the part of the cute little girl coaxing her daddy into spoiling her with a cookie before supper. Again I was playing games with God instead of approaching Him from a mature, trusting relationship.

The wife portrayed in the sixties book *Fascinating Womanhood* was one who had to tease, coax, and, if necessary, deceive her husband in order to get her way. I was approaching God in much the same way.

My prayers were making God out to be capricious, like the gods of the Greeks and Romans. "Thy will be done." My lips might have been saying "Thy will be done," but my heart was saying "*My* will be done." Like a trapeze artist hedging her bets by using a safety net, I was using the phrase to save face, should the Lord choose not to heal me.

In other words, I was "wavering," as the apostle James described in his book. Even as I squeezed shut my eyes and kept repeating the words "I believe!" I felt more like the little girl in the Christmas classic *Miracle on 34th Street,* believing in the existence of Santa Claus, than like a child of God trusting her Father to keep His word.

"Father," I prayed, "You said to ask and it would be given, seek and I would find, knock and it would be opened to me. Well, I'm asking, seeking, and knocking."

Again I was directed not to human beings, but to the Word. I found promises of healing throughout Scripture.

God describes Himself as the "Healer." In Exodus 23:25 He promises that if we worship Him (give Him praise), He will take away our diseases. He says, "I Am the healer of your disease." Not I was, or I will be, but I Am. Psalm 103 reaffirms God's promise of healing. And as if to add a divine stamp of authenticity to His Word, 2 Corinthians 1:20 says, "For no matter how many promises God has made, they are 'Yes' in Christ" (NIV). Yes!

"Father, I know You keep Your word. So, as I see it, Lord," I prayed, "You have three choices here. You can heal me instantly, heal me over time, or heal me when You take me home. You choose which choice will best bring glory and honor to Your name. Regardless of the method You choose, I want to thank You for giving me my promised healing."

From then on I prayed, not begging to be healed, but asking for ways I could glorify the Saviour's name through my disease. He opened all sorts of doors. I met and conversed with so many people who were fighting the same battles. I shared my discoveries with them; they shared with me.

Morning and evening when I took my asthma medications I thanked God for causing the creators of the medicines to discover the chemicals that eased my pain. I also thanked God for healing me in His time.

Then one evening Richard and I were in Los Angeles for some teachers' meetings, and we attended an interdenominational prayer service. During the song service, while we were standing and singing "My Jesus, I Love Thee," God reached down and touched me with the force of a football linebacker. I sat down with a thud, the breath totally knocked out of me.

He healed my scarred lungs. He removed my asthma. I left the meeting knowing without a doubt that I'd been healed. I didn't take my asthma medication that night or in the morning. When I returned home and told a respiratory therapist friend what had happened, he said, "If you hadn't been healed you probably would have been hospitalized within 28 hours for going without your medications."

That was two years ago. Today I can shout! Today I can run! Today I can sing full voice, "To God be the glory, great things He hath done," and continues to do for His children.

My praise facilitates the Holy Spirit's action in my body as well as my soul. As one preacher put it, "the Holy Spirit moves on the wings of praise." By offering to my heavenly Father my sacrifice of praise, I open the door to His blessings.

The following story demonstrates an interesting example of the incredible value of the sacrifice of praise. A small commuter plane, carrying four relief missionaries heading for the furthest outpost of eastern Russia, developed engine trouble over the Bering Sea. When one engine coughed, sputtered, then stopped, the passengers looked warily toward the pilot for encouragement. The pilot struggled to restart the engine. Suddenly the other engine coughed.

"Put on those parachutes!" the pilot shouted. The passengers obeyed. The second engine coughed again, then sputtered and stopped.

After giving their location to the Coast Guard in Anchorage, the pilot instructed his passengers on the operation of their parachutes while strapping on his own chute. Don, the medical doctor of the team, mumbled the pilot's instructions as he leaped into the turbulent Bering Sea.

He remembered the statistics for staying alive in such frigid water—13 minutes. *Thirteen minutes of grace,* he thought desperately. *Not much time for a Coast Guard plane to rescue us.* "Oh, Lord," he gasped, plunging into the ice-cold saltwater.

Bobbing to the surface, he found himself singing a psalm, not the twenty-third for comfort or the ninety-first for deliverance, but Psalm 118:24—definitely not the psalm I would think of at such a moment. Catching his breath, his teeth chattering from the cold, he shouted, "'This is the day the Lord has made; let us rejoice and be glad' [NIV]!"

Don threw back his head and laughed. *How outrageous!* he thought. His companions, bobbing nearby on the surface of the water, looked at him incredulously. Don sang the chorus a second time, this time with gusto. He continued singing the little chorus throughout the magical 13 minutes, stopping only to listen for the drone of a rescue plane.

Fifteen minutes passed. Twenty. As Don sang, he pictured his wife and children, home in southern California, playing by the pool in their backyard. He brushed the thought aside and sang. Occasionally a wave would crest, and Don would lose sight of the others. When the waters ebbed, he'd count heads to be certain all were still afloat.

Twenty-five minutes. Thirty. Forty-five. Don sang the simple psalm again and again. When—totally numb—he no longer felt pain in his feet and legs, he sang.

An hour from the time the pilot called out his first SOS, the victims of the plane crash heard the drone of an airplane. Ten minutes later all were safely on board the Coast Guard rescue plane and heading back to Anchorage.

Was it a miracle or luck that a plane was patrolling in the general vicinity when the emergency call went out? Was it a miracle or healthy constitutions that prevented any of the five survivors from losing toes, feet, or legs, or even surviving past the 13-minute grace period? Was it because of Don's choice of music, or was there magic in the psalmist's words? Don doesn't claim to know. Would the story of his ordeal have been as inspiring if he'd drowned before help could arrive? Definitely not to Don.

But what Don *did* know is that he didn't consciously "choose" to sing that particular psalm out of all the hymns of praise that he knew. He didn't plunge into the icy surf thinking *Now, let me see, what psalm would be appropriate for this occasion?*

To Don, praise was as natural as breathing. The words sprang into his mind out of habit—the habit of praise. He'd made it a habit to live in the Spirit of abundance. If Don had been living in the spirit of scarcity, he might have looked around at the hopelessness of his situation and sung the old country-western tune "Oh, Lonesome Me." Instead he automatically sang, "This the day that the Lord has made . . ." From experience, Don was confident that God knew all about his predicament. The icy bath didn't come as a surprise to the Creator. He had everything under control.

"Let us rejoice and be glad in it." Because Don knew that his day rested safely in God's hands, he had no cause to fret. Shiver, yes; but worry, no. Don could rejoice and be glad, despite the circumstances. He didn't think through the logic of his choice of music. He spontaneously sang the words and the tune he had memorized years earlier.

"Let us educate our hearts and lips to speak the praise of God for His matchless love. Let us educate our souls to be hopeful and to abide in the light shining from the cross of Calvary. Never should we forget that we are children of the heavenly King, sons and daughters of the Lord of hosts." [2]

Trapped in his worst nightmare, Don never doubted that he was God's much-loved son. His confidence in his Father never swayed. His song of praise was a battle cry against the enemy of death and a salute to the King of kings and Lord of lords. As the subzero temperatures leached life-sustaining warmth from his body, he tapped into God's wellspring of joy and found comfort and peace. If Don had concentrated on his discomfort, he would have drowned within the 13-minute grace period. But by concentrating on the goodness of God, he allowed God to save him.

We may never find ourselves battling the frigid temperatures of the Bering Sea, but Jesus warned us that we'd see our share of troubles in this life. We can choose to wail and berate God for every injury, real or imagined; or we can remind ourselves that our Father knows best. Our attitude toward our problems determines our success or failure as a child of God.

Immediately after her regular visit to her psychologist, Nina attended a local women's meeting at which I was speaking. It had been a breakthrough session for the woman, but one that had left her shaken by her memories of her abusive childhood. As she entered the meeting, she vowed that if I said one word about family, especially parents, she would get up and leave.

Her chagrin grew when I not only mentioned God as our loving parent, but focused my entire presentation on the parent/child relationship and about praising God in all circumstances. Worse yet, she couldn't carry out her vow to leave, because she was seated back in a corner of the room, with no easy exit.

After the closing prayer Nina hurried out as quickly as possible. Then, in the solitude of her automobile, she decided to "try the praise thing." But for the life of her she couldn't think of one praise text or praise song. The only word that came to her mind was "alleluia," derivative of "hallelujah." In a feeble voice she croaked the first notes of the repetitive chorus, "Alleluia." It sounded more like a funeral dirge than a song of praise.

When she finished singing the song, she sang it again, and then again. Slowly her mind opened. Her song, no matter how feeble, freed God's mighty fighting force to rout Satan and his nasty cohorts. By the time she reached her home, she'd sung "every praise chorus I'd ever learned."

Months later Nina shared her story with me. "And, you know what?" she said. "It works the same way every time, no matter how discouraged I am."

Praising God in the face of adversity makes no sense from an earthly perspective. It's upside down and backwards. When we praise God we are giving up something—for sacrifice means surrender. What we are sacrificing is the right to the blessings we think we deserve. We are also sacrificing our human desire to understand everything instantly.

My sacrifice of praise can be the catalyst for turning evil events and situations into good ones. Catherine Marshall compared it with the process a photographer goes through developing negatives into beautiful prints. When a negative is held up to the light, all objects are reversed: black is white, white is black. Once plunged into the developing chemicals, the "latent image" is revealed in the print—darkness turns to light. Just as the photographer has to wait for the chemicals to work, we too must wait—meanwhile continuing to praise—while the Spirit does His work.[3]

---

[1] Don Matzat, *Truly Transformed: Breaking Through . . . Stubborn Habits, Fear of Failure, Thoughts of Confusion and Anxiety* (Eugene, Oreg.: Harvest House Publishers, 1992), p. 67.

[2] Ellen White, *Life at Its Best* (Mountain View, Calif.: Pacific Press Pub. Assn., 1964), p. 157.

[3] Catherine Marshall, *Something More* (New York: McGraw-Hill Book Company, 1974), pp. 32, 33.

CHAPTER SIX

Living in the Perspective of Praise

What I hate about modern technology is that the equipment I purchase always becomes outdated the day I make my last payment. Also, technophiles seem compelled to upgrade the equipment the day the machine enters the house. My dear "tekki" husband has hauled me, kicking and screaming, from an Apple computer to a Commodore to Macintoshes 1, 2, and 3. The resulting adjustments I must make, whether to a new program or a new machine, involves the retraining of *me!* A frustrating inconvenience, especially if I have writing deadlines to meet.

Another thing I've observed is that the thickness of the accompanying manual is in direct and opposite proportion to the clarity with which the manual is written! I know full well that if I intend to enjoy the benefits of my new acquisition, I will need to take the time to read that manual. This admission is from the woman who, when learning to sew, never read the pattern directions until she'd sewn a sleeve or zipper in backwards.

God's "abundant life" program also comes with an instruction manual—the Bible. I knew that if I didn't take the time to read and learn how praise really works, I'd never discover all the fantastic benefits. Worse yet, I'd be in for another roller-coaster ride. And at the end of the "ride" I would disembark more discouraged and disillusioned than before.

The manual clearly teaches that the Christian life is a transformed life from the inside out. "If anyone is in Christ, there is a new creation" (2 Corinthians 5:17, NRSV). We are "born again" by the "living and enduring word of God" (1 Peter 1:23, NIV). This isn't a onetime event, but an ongoing process of changes in our lives.

First Peter 1:18 says that we were "redeemed from the empty way of life [spirit of scarcity] handed down to [us] by [our] forefathers" (NIV). *If I am already redeemed from the world of scarcity and fear, why am I still living it?* I wondered. I didn't want to settle for only the future kingdom of God and miss out on the best part of what God can do in my life today.

In addition, I'd been working so hard on my own salvation that I had little energy left to be concerned with the salvation of others. Hence, my witness was ineffectual. Until I experienced for myself the freedom of which Jesus spoke in John 8:32, I could not begin to loose the chains imprisoning my brothers and sisters. Until my life shone with incredible joy flaming from within, I had no viable light to give.

"I come that you might have life and have it more abundantly!" Abundant! In the hyperbole! I wanted God's abundance poured out on me, not in dribbles and sun showers but gully-washer great. I wanted my faith to glow torch-bright. I wanted my love for others to surpass the high-society, "peck on the cheek" variety. I wanted to give spiritual "kisses" that would knock the world's socks off!

That's the abundance I craved—peace instead of fear, love in place of anger, and joy that bubbled from me like a Yellowstone Park geyser. The changes I'd already experienced were exciting. Suddenly I found people praising God everywhere I went. Finding it so often in my favorite old hymns surprised me. Fanny Crosby understood praise when she wrote "Blessed Assurance." Reginald Heber's "Holy, Holy, Holy" took on new significance for me.

I remember the first time I viewed the painting of the second coming of Jesus hanging in the foyer of the Milo Academy church. At first that's all I saw, the familiar scene of Jesus coming in the clouds with His angels and with people gazing up into the sky. But as I studied it closer, I began to see people's faces in the rocks, in the bushes, and in the clouds. It was as if Someone had "turned on the light" inside my mind. Once my eyes picked up the hidden messages, I could never look at the painting again in the same way. And whenever visitors toured the campus, I had to share with them my incredible discovery.

I felt a similar excitement when I began praising. The Holy Spirit opened my eyes and my world began to change. Verses that had previously been obscure and meaningless now burst from the sacred pages, clear and alive. For the first time in my life I really craved the Word of God. I'd sniffed the heady aroma of new wine, sipped its sweet bouquet, and I wanted more. "Lord, I want it all—now! Your kingdom, Your presence, the Holy Spirit's power—everything! I won't settle for less!"

In my search for God and His kingdom I suddenly "saw" the exciting truth of Psalm 22:3. "But thou art holy," David wrote, "O thou that inhabitest the praise of Israel." My God inhabits the praise of His people? He lives in the atmosphere of my praise? The concept leaped off the onionskin pages of my Bible and into my imagination.

If God inhabits the praises of His people, then when we praise Him the devil and his imps have to flee. Satan can't tolerate the presence of a perfect Being. We have declared our allegiance to the God of order and peace and there is no room for the father of discord and strife to remain.

The opposite is also true. When our attitude is one of complaining and whining, God must leave. When we choose to live in the spirit of scarcity, God's pure, sinless nature cannot tolerate the presence of evil. We have chosen to give our allegiance to the father of lies and will live in his darkness (see Romans 1:21).

I truly desired to live in God's presence and to have His presence live in me. But to do so, I could no longer cosset my bitterness, my rage and anger against those who'd hurt me.

"Get rid of all bitterness, rage and anger, brawling and slander, along with every form of malice" (Ephesians 4:31, 32, NIV). I'd tried for years to do this and failed. But now, to know that I had a choice revolutionized my thinking.

~

"[I] have not received the spirit of the world but the Spirit who is from God, that [I] may understand what God has freely given us" (1 Corinthians 2:12, NIV). I assure you, whining is in my nature. I come from a royal line of blue-blood complainers. My right to choose whether or not to complain happens not through my power but through the power of a living God.

When I received the spirit of daughtership, and by Christ cried "Daddy, Father," I took on the family name and acquired the right to choose to live either in the ghetto of scarcity and fear, or in the neighborhood of abundance and praise (see Romans 8:12-17). Before my adoption, I had no choice. I lived a prisoner in the ghetto of fear.

I wage a real battle when I fight the battle for the control of my attitude. I am bombarded on all sides by the demons of discouragement, of despair, of divorce, of cynicism, and suicide. These creatures are not figments of my overwrought imagination. They are real beings, able to enter my home, my church, and my mind by invitation only (Ephesians 6:12).

And nothing galls Satan more than for me to enjoy the pleasures he lost and can never regain. The last thing he wants is for God's children to grasp the concept of praise, to discover that they, through the power of the Holy Spirit, can consistently defeat him.

Living in the Spirit of abundance and praise turns the raging lion of 1 Peter 5:8 into an aging lion. However, while his teeth may rot and fall out, his claws can still maim and destroy if I'm foolish enough to get too close to him. I have no reason to fear the evil one when I surround myself by praise, the natural protection of the Holy Spirit.

~

In Romans 8:6 Paul said, "The mind of sinful [woman] is death" (NIV). Think about the life-threatening diseases humans battle today. Most are brought on, or at the least, aggravated by stress, anger, and bitterness. Personally, every physical problem I endure today can be traced back to stress.

The text continues by saying, "But the mind controlled by the Spirit is life and peace." The previous verse reads "Those who live according to the sinful nature have their minds set on what that nature desires [spirit of scarcity — never enough!]; but those who live with the Spirit have their minds set on what the Spirit desires [thanksgiving and praise]."

As adopted children of God, we've been set apart (1 Peter 2:9) as members of His royal priesthood for the divine purpose of praising Him. What makes us unique and special is not the clothes we wear or don't wear; or the food we eat or don't eat. It's not the songs we sing or the scripture we recite. The hedge of protection mentioned by Job — the one that separates and protects us from the world of scarcity and fear — is our attitude for living.

I'm a people watcher. Long layovers in distant airports give me the opportunity to watch the antics of my fellow travelers. On their faces I most often see anxiety, boredom, and irritation. And why not? Traveling is stressful. Only the occasional face reflects a spirit of peace and contentment.

I pursued this habit to extreme on one of my flights out of the San Francisco airport. After a long wait in the terminal, we boarded our plane and taxied onto the runway. On cue, our plane sped down the runway. As the wheels lifted from the concrete, an engine directly outside my window exploded — noise, flames, smoke, the works. My first thought wasn't *Oh no, I'm going to die.* Instead I glanced about me, recording in my memory the terrified expressions on the faces of my fellow travelers. Now, that's hard-core people watching! I probably did it thinking I could write about the experience later — if I survived the crash.

To relieve any anxiety, I'll finish the story. The nose of the plane dropped. The plane bounced on its tires a couple times and slowed to a stop. The pilot's satin-smooth, reassuring tones filled the cabin. "Ladies and gentlemen, we seem to be experiencing minor technical difficulties and will be returning to the gate at this time." Minor technical difficulties! Two seconds later and we would have found ourselves bouncing down the emergency slide or worse.

The sharp contrast between terror and peace that I saw on my fellow passengers' faces will stay in my mind forever. I especially remember the older woman sitting next to me. As we limped back to the gate, she looked at me and smiled.

"A little scary, huh?" I volunteered.

"Yes, but God had everything under control, didn't He?"

Instantly we were sisters, bonded together by the blood of our Elder Brother, Jesus Christ. Tears misted my eyes, and I returned her big smile. "Praise God, He surely did."

Living in the Spirit of abundance means believing that God will keep His promises. "Ye shall know the truth"—the truth is I can successfully live in the Spirit of abundance through the perspective of praise every day of my life.

The Old Testament prophet warned, "My people are destroyed for lack of knowledge" (Hosea 4:6). How sad when the key to abundant living is available to every child of God. Praise is such a simple concept. Yet people die never knowing how victorious they could have been had they chosen to live in the Spirit of abundance.

The Saviour said that we must "become as little children" to enter the kingdom of God (Matthew 18:3). Children naturally express praise. Watch a young child romping in a field of daisies or studying the creatures living in a tidal pool. Somewhere in the course of growing, that childlike joy gets smothered by sin, guilt, and supposed obligations.

~

Praising sets us free from the bondage of our problems and from our load of guilt. When we praise, we open the way for God's love to be poured out on us in heavenly abundance. All of heaven is at our fingertips. "Mercy, peace and love [could now be mine] in abundance" (Jude 2, NIV), along with faith, courage, joy, and healing. And as a bonus, all doubts we might have had as to whose children we are are gone.

~

Was this the missing piece of the puzzle for which I'd been seeking? Was this the Source of the abundant peace about which the apostles wrote? I tested it, and it proved reliable, just like all of the other God-made promises in His Holy Word.

Even though I had so much more to learn, I could confidently say that the joy in the journey was worth every effort. I no longer needed to live as the "Gentiles do, in the futility of their thinking" (Ephesians 4:17, NIV). For I did not receive "the spirit of the world but the Spirit who is from God." I could finally begin to "understand what God has freely given" me (1 Corinthians 2:12, NIV).

My Dad is an abundant God—not only "was" or "will be," but "is." He's the Father of lights. He's the Father of all good and precious gifts. As His darling daughter, I can throw back my shoulders, level my chin, and smile confidently into the face of the existing kingdom of scarcity, for I live in a better neighborhood. I inhabit a sphere of praise that transcends distance, time, and circumstances. There's plenty of room for you too if you choose.

"Blessed are those who have learned to acclaim you, who walk in the light of your presence, O Lord" (Psalm 89:15, NIV).

CHAPTER SEVEN

Daddy Dearest

W hen I hear the word "daddy," I remember family picnics at Pine Lake Beach, water fights on the lawn—garden hose and all. I see a short, round man, dressed in Bermuda shorts, sandals, and a white athletic undershirt, mowing the lawn or rocking in a cane-back chair on the front porch. I see the same man in paint-splattered work overalls, standing on a scaffold, repainting the front gable of our local church. My earliest recollection is of my dad sitting in a dark-blue-upholstered wing-backed chair and reading the evening paper. A later memory is of seeing my 18-month-old daughter Rhonda lead my 200-pound father by his pinkie finger to the basement stairs, asking for a "minnum." "Minnums," more easily identified as popsicles, were kept in the basement freezer.

One of my last memories is of that same little girl, a few years later, asking her grandpa to take her for a walk to see the horses. His answer still lives in her heart and in mine. "I can't right now, honey," he said. "I'm too sick. But someday I promise that you and I will take a walk together in heaven to see the horses. OK?" She still remembers his promise. That's the "daddy" I see.

So when I think of God as my Father, or even more personally, as my daddy (Romans 8:15), I experience good, strong, positive emotions and tears of gratitude.

For some men and women, however, their tears are not tears of nostalgia, but of anger, frustration, and resentment.

Their memories of "daddy" are distorted by humiliation and abuse. The resulting dysfunction touches every aspect of their lives, including the way they interpret God, the Father.

Bill Ritchie, pastor of the Crossroads Community Church in Vancouver, Washington, tells in his book *A Dad Who Loves You: Experiencing the Joy of a Perfect Father* of a survey he took of his congregation. He asked, "What comes to mind when you hear the word 'dad'? What kind of relationship did you have with your dad when you were growing up?"

He was stunned by the response he received. "Words cannot express the avalanche of emotion that my little survey generated," he writes. "Within a few days I had received hundreds of replies. And while a few wrote only a couple words, the vast majority poured out their souls. Some people had such deep feelings that they sent back eight pages of material, typed and single-spaced . . . I was unprepared for the ferocity of the reactions. . . . More than once I found written, 'I have never told anybody about this before. You have no idea how much this means to me to get this off my chest.'" [1]

Ritchie determined from his survey that *dads have one of the greatest effects on us of anyone we will ever meet.* The effect continues whether he's alive or dead.

Of the fundamental Christians surveyed, 37.5 percent had experienced terrific relationships with their fathers. Another 37.5 percent experienced bad relationships. They added terms like stormy, hate, rejection, embarrassment, shame, violence, a wife-beating child molester. Some said, "I was never good enough for him," or "He was the warden and I the prisoner." [2]

And for the last 25 percent, their relationship with their dad had been "indifferent"—either he wasn't there for them or they never knew him or he wasn't interested in them. Some admitted that they were always seeking his approval and affection, but never seemed to get it. [3]

What does this mean in the context of God? Sandra, a young friend of mine, admitted not being able to "think" of

God as a father. She cringed every time the term was used. "I hated my dad," she explained. "He was a pitiful, alcohol-soaked excuse of a human being! Not only was he a wife-beater, but he molested all three of us girls."

At a women's retreat a middle-aged woman cornered me after my "Daughters of Destiny" presentation and said, "Something came up at the last minute, so my daughter couldn't attend your talk, and I'm so glad it did." She continued before I could react. "She was terribly abused by her father. Your presentation would have made her fighting mad. God doesn't really expect her to forgive him, does He?"

I swallowed hard and prayed for wisdom before answering. "Our God is a compassionate God. He won't push your daughter faster than she's ready to move. He'll give her the time and the grace she needs as long as she trusts Him to do so."

At another retreat Evelyn, a 78-year-old widow and the daughter of a pastor, burst into tears as I spoke. Her friends reached out in love and held her in their arms until the end of the meeting. Evelyn told me later, "I'd buried the memories of the abuse I suffered at the hand of my father all these years. He's been dead more than 50 years, and he's still getting through to me! I thought I'd gained victory over the hate I felt years ago." She pounded her clenched fist on the table before her. "He had no right to do the terrible things he did to me. He had no right!"

Her entire life had been affected by her attitude toward her father—her relationship with men, her husband, their marriage, her parenting skills, her self-image, and her spiritual growth. She saw God as a self-seeking authority figure who was not above using force to get His way. She saw Him in the only way she knew to view a father—as a being that makes unfair demands on His children, one that can't be pleased no matter how hard they try. God was, to her, a sadistic Deity, only to be feared.

Evelyn's experience isn't isolated. Some of you relate all too well. If your father was distant or uninterested in you,

you probably find that perception reoccurring in your relationship with God. The distorted images you have of your father will make it tremendously difficult for you to understand who and what God really is. This distortion can keep you from experiencing the joy and the peace that is your right as a child of the "perfect Dad." It can rob you of the health and the happiness and the wholeness you were designed to possess. It can prevent you from ever finding that new life in the kingdom of God. The good news is it doesn't have to.

"Easy for you to say!" you may say. "You weren't the by-product of your dad's drunken orgy! The damage is done. What can I do about it now?"

My reply is "Be comforted. That's what being born again is all about. It's a second chance, a chance to 'grow up' with the perfect Father." John 1:12, 13 tells us, "To all who received him, to those who believed in his name, he gave the *right* to become children of God—children born not of natural descent, nor of human decision or of a husband's will, but born of God" (NIV). That's fabulous! Utterly fabulous!

We're all in the same dirty clothes basket when it comes to distorted views of God. We all need a new and improved Tide in our lives. And remember, even the best of dads fail at one time or another. Being a shy, quiet person, my dad didn't always understand his bombastic, hyperbolic daughter. He worked long hard hours to keep me in poodle skirts and sweater sets. As a result, he wasn't always there for me when I needed him.

For others, perhaps their fathers' expectations were too high, exerting the undue pressure to perform or conform. Perhaps your dad flew off the handle, overreacted, and lost his cool too easily. Perhaps he found it difficult to demonstrate his love, or didn't know how to listen when you needed him. Whatever, all fathers—being human—at times fail to live up to the perfect image of the perfect dad.

To change our attitude about our heavenly Father, we must come to "see" that the heavenly Father's character is not the same as our earthly father's. The Bible shows us what God as a perfect dad is all about. Psalm 37:4 tells us that our Dad delights in granting us the "desires of [our] heart." We see Him as being incredibly patient. How many times did He tolerate Israel's little rebellions before He moved in to clean up their messes? He sent Jesus to earth to give us a flesh-and-blood example of the "perfect dad." Through the Saviour we can see that God is faithful and constant. He keeps His promises. He loves unconditionally and expresses that love in every way possible.

"You will seek me and find me when you seek me with all your heart" (Jeremiah 29:13, NIV). We must first desire a relationship with the Father, with all our hearts—that's the secret.

When you read John 1:12, did you note the word "right"? He gives us the right to become His children because we believe in Him and because we accept the sacrifice of Jesus Christ. Our "birthright" (born again) is more than a bunch of concepts typed out on paper, or doctrines to memorize for a test, or catchphrases to banter about at church potlucks.

When we've been born again, we become the "apple of [God's] eye" (Psalm 17:8), translated by some biblical scholars as "darling daughters." Once we are God's darling daughters, we are protected by the presence of the Holy Spirit living in us. And while Satan may have the ability to destroy us, he no longer has the authority to do so.

When I was a child, a boy name Tommy Collins lived across the alleyway from us. He and one of his buddies loved to torment my best friend, Patty, and me by throwing rocks at us. I still bear the scars to prove it. Patty and I ran for the house when we saw Tommy coming.

One day I didn't see him approaching until I felt the first pebble hit the side my head. This time, instead of fleeing, I stood up, placed my hands defiantly on my hips, and shouted, "You go away, Tommy Collins. You're a big bully! I don't like you!" I knew something he didn't.

Tommy and the boy with him just laughed. "What are you going to do about it?" Tommy asked, swaggering over to where I stood.

I stiffened my spine and further narrowed the gap between us. "I'll tell your mama, that's what!"

Suddenly his face blanched. His friend backed up a few feet, then bolted down the alleyway. I recognized my advantage and moved in closer. But Tommy's eyes weren't focused on me. They were focused on something or someone more frightening. My daddy had rounded the corner of the garage wielding an impressive yardstick in his hands. This was back in the days when the adults on the block assumed the role of parent when necessary.

A few choice words of advice from my daddy, and Tommy disappeared down the alleyway, never to bully us again. I was my daddy's darling daughter, and he wasn't about to let Tommy Collins bully her around. That day my five-foot-eight-inch daddy stood 10 feet tall in my eyes. Growing in Jesus is similar in many ways to the way children grow physically. The eyes of newborns need time to develop before they are capable of recognizing their parents' faces. What a thrill it was for me the first time Rhonda, our elder daughter, followed my finger with her eyes. I also remember Richard's excitement when she first smiled at him. That night a proud father called the grandparents with the news! I marvel at how tolerant they were of his boasting.

To Richard, Rhonda was the brightest, most talented, most beautiful baby ever born. And she knew he loved her. Somehow she sensed when it was time for him to come home from work. The moment his footsteps sounded on the walkway, she'd begin bobbing up and down in the playpen. I'd barely get a perfunctory peck before he'd sweep her into his arms. Rhonda didn't know what it meant to be a "daddy," but she did know who he was.

A darling daughter starts her new life in Christ as a newborn and will go through spiritual growing pains much like the growing pains in the physical world of a child. At first the spiritual infant can't "see" the face of her Daddy too clearly, but as she matures, she begins to see and recognize His face in every aspect of her life. And like our daughter Rhonda, she finds joy just being in her Daddy's presence.

Babies learn to talk by babbling at first, sounds that make little sense to anyone. Spiritual infants babble nonsensical, unsound ideas occasionally, and Daddy God recognizes their babbling as attempts to communicate with Him, even when they don't have all their theological syllables straight.

We must relearn how to talk to our Father. This is where the praising comes in. He also teaches us how to talk with our brothers and sisters. We learn to encourage, not discourage; to build up instead of tear down; and to comfort, not criticize. This is a difficult lesson to learn.

We must learn, as children of the heavenly King, how to talk to ourselves. You know what I mean. You make a mistake, you spill spaghetti sauce on your favorite skirt, and what comes next?

"You stupid jerk!" you yell at yourself. "You know you should have changed clothing before you . . ." We wouldn't think of pouring out such verbal abuse on our spouses or our children, but we bombard ourselves mercilessly.

When Jesus warned in Matthew 18:6 of hurting one of His little ones, He was also speaking of injuring His spiritual babies. Castigating ourselves over our humanity tears down and destroys the beautiful person God put inside of each of us. People are more often destroyed by themselves than by others.

My own mother could never completely accept the fact that she could possibly be worthy of love. The scars from her childhood scored so deeply into her psyche that she received every declaration of love with a hint of skepticism. While she accepted the abstract truth of Jesus' love and sacrifice for all of us, she hesitated to believe the sacrifice would have been made personally for her alone, if necessary.

In 1 John 3:1 it says, "How great is the love the Father lavishes on us, that we should be called the children of God" (NIV). Lavishes! I love that word. The Father *lavishes* His love on us. As a parent, I can almost understand. I adore buying gifts for my girls and now my sons-in-law. I love pawing through dozens of clothing racks for just the right dress or suit, then searching through the accessories department for the right scarf, pin, hat, or shoes to complete an outfit for one of my daughters.

Examining everything later at home is also part of my pleasure. But my real joy comes on Christmas morning when they open their packages and I hear their "oohs" and "aahs" and squeals of delight. And every time I see them wearing the clothing I purchased, I relive the pleasure again. Yes, I can understand the pleasure God receives when He lavishes us with His love.

Some Christians believe that one's possessions are the measuring rod for their worthiness in God's eyes. That a great job, good food, and a late-model car are God's affirmation of the person. And they suspect that a person experiencing financial loss should search his or her soul for the sin that caused this reversal. Tell that to Noble Alexander, Corrie ten Boom, Mother Teresa, and so many more beautiful Christians who trod the path of poverty.

Any parent will tell you that lavishing love is more than giving "things." Each child is unique and must be treated as such.

Our younger daughter, Kelli, loved being held by her daddy and having her back rubbed. The moment Richard sat down in his recliner in the evening, Kelli would scramble onto his lap and beg for a back rub. As she grew, the custom continued whenever she was upset, had a bad day at school, or just had a bad day in general. Now, it wasn't that her older sister, Rhonda, didn't like to be hugged (she did), but we could bestow hugs only on her terms.

We moved away from our home of seven years at the beginning of Kelli's junior year of high school. When alumni weekend arrived at her old school, she and Rhonda arranged to attend the ceremony with friends while Richard and I stayed home.

The phone call came around midnight. The hysterical caller babbled something about a car accident and someone being killed. My husband tried to quiet the girl enough to decipher the details, but the girl would not be quieted. We tried to contact the school officials, but got only busy signals. Within 15 minutes of the call, we jumped into the car and set out for the school, 200 miles away. Three and a half hours later we located our shaken daughters at a friend's house.

After learning the details of the accident in which Kelli had been riding and her best friend had been killed, we drove to the local hospital to have Kelli checked for a possible concussion. Rhonda, who'd not been along on the tragic ride, asked to drive home. She was too keyed up to sleep. I climbed in the front seat to keep her alert. In the rear seat Kelli curled up like a 3-year-old across her daddy's lap. Frightened and weepy, she whispered, "Rub my back, Daddy."

All the way home to Portland, Richard rubbed Kelli's back and soothed her with his presence. Later he told me that as he'd felt the road cinders in her hair and smelled the odor of gasoline on her clothing, he'd realized how close we'd come to losing her.

As tired as he was, an entire bottle of sleeping pills could not have kept him from meeting Kelli's needs. He was there for her. That's love. That's lavished love. Yet it's only a smidgen of the love God showers on us when we let Him.

God's love allows us to grow safely in Him, to learn to trust Him. When He says that all things work out for my good (see Romans 8:28) I can believe it. Though I can't understand at the moment, one day I will.

We know that no matter what happens, God will be there for us. We may fall and scrape our knees, run our pantyhose, maybe even break our hearts, but He'll be beside us to pick us up and dust us off and set us back on our feet once more. "Nothing touches us that has not passed through the hands of my heavenly Father."[4]

As parents we all "suffered" through our children's growing years. We beamed with pride at piano recitals. We endured lessons on the violin, French horn, flute, and, horror of horrors, the percussion instruments. We kissed away thousands of tears with wise counsel like "Don't worry, honey; you won't always have zits."

As a teenager Kelli would get perturbed when I'd sing to her the words of Kenny Rogers' hit "You Are So Beautiful to Me."

"Of course you'd say that. You're my mother!" Despite her protests, I am confident that the message got through — "You, my daughter, are much loved."

As His adopted daughter, I know that Father God loves me, freckles and all. He recognizes my need to mature at my own pace. Just as human parents accept their children's individuality, so God accepts our specialness. He guides us along different pathways and corrects our mistakes individually.

When I was in labor with Rhonda, I shared the labor room with another woman, the mother of three. She'd been in labor six hours before I arrived. She advised me between contractions, "Don't be surprised, honey, if your first labor goes 12 to 14 hours. Mine went 10."

Fate and the variances of female anatomy played in my favor. I delivered 45 minutes later. As they wheeled me toward the delivery room, she cried, "That's not fair. I was here first!"

Pregnancy, childbirth, and parenting are never fair. What is fair about giving birth to a malformed baby or a baby with cystic fibrosis or without sight? From the moment of conception, parenting is a risk. And not just in infancy, but at each step in the process. Yet generation after generation we continue to take the gamble. Why? For the same reason God created Eve. He knew before He first drew His finger through the dust of Eden that she and the marvelous man sleeping by her side would disappoint Him. In spite of knowing that fact, God created man and woman because He already loved them beyond words.

While holding the infant Rhonda in my arms, I would take her tiny fingers in mine and imagine them skilled enough to play chopsticks. Today those fingers entertain large audiences with inspiring renditions of Mozart, Bartok, and Beethoven.

God does the same with us. Even before we take our first breath, our loving heavenly Parent sees us, not as the immature brats or wimpy cowards we will sometimes be, but as the beautiful and talented women into which we will blossom through the warmth of His love.

---

[1] Bill Ritchie, *A Dad Who Loves You: Experiencing the Joy of a Perfect Father* (Sisters, Oreg.: Multnomah Press Books, 1992), p. 12.

[2] *Ibid.*, p. 14.

[3] *Ibid.*, p. 23.

[4] Charles R. Swindoll, *Improving Your Serve: The Art of Unselfish Living* (Waco, Tex.: Key-Word Books, 1981), p. 189.

CHAPTER EIGHT

The Promise of Praise

I gave my community college writing class an assignment: to jot down an original book idea, plot it out, and present it to the class. On the night the assignment was due, I listened to a variety of political intrigue plots, sci-fi scenarios, and romance yarns. But one particular book idea fascinated me.

The story began on the undisclosed estate of a wealthy Eastern industrialist. Concerned by the irresponsible behavior of his grandchildren, the crusty old man had gathered the family together for a picnic on the lawn. After the meal, he proposed his plan. He would send each of the grandchildren out to make their way in the world on their own. "Once you finish your education, I, along with your parents, of course, will choose a city where you will reside for 10 years under an assumed name.

"During those 10 years you must not use the family name to get ahead. For that matter, you can't tell anyone your real name. You must make it on your own. You will be allowed to come home for visits, and I will give you a set sum of money to get you started. If at the end of 10 years you have made a success of yourself, you may return home and we will have a place for you in the family business with all the rights and privileges thereof. However, if you've messed up your life . . ."

Thinking it good potential for a novel, the class members bombarded her with ideas for exciting twists and turns that she could develop into her story. Somewhere during the discussion we learned we weren't talking fiction. This was her story. She'd been sent to the Northwest to prove herself.

I'm so grateful my Father God isn't like that. He never sends me out into the cruel world to "make it on my own." When He did send His disciples out two by two to share the good news, He promised, "Lo, I am with you always" (Matthew 28:20, RSV).

He never forbade His sons or His daughters to use His name. Quite the contrary, He wants us to tell the world that we're His. When we "do good," Zephaniah 3:17 says He brags on us. In *The Living Bible* it says He sings over us like a choir. Imagine God singing a psalm of praise in 12-part harmony to honor you!

Our Father made a covenant with each of us, a promise, a contract. That contract is found in Psalm 103. I call it the promise of praise. "Praise the Lord, O my soul, and forget not all his benefits" (verse 2, NIV). That's our side of the bargain—to praise Him and remember all the things He's done for us.

On His side, He makes six pledges. First, He promises to forgive all our sins. Peter, Mary Magdalene, and the centurion each stood at the foot of the cross. Like millions of sinners before and after, the centurion didn't know until he came face-to-face with Jesus that he needed forgiveness and salvation. When he met the truth in the person of Jesus, he declared, "Truly this man was the Son of God" (Mark 15:39). Mary represents the sinner who falls again and again, yet claims the forgiveness Jesus gave. Peter symbolizes a sinner like me—one that walked and talked with the Master, one that knew Him well and claimed to be faithful, but still denied Him. Each needed forgiveness that day. Each had to accept the gift of forgiveness made possible at the cross.

God promises that the instant a sinner asks for forgiveness, He will forgive. His answer is never no or maybe, but always "'Yes' in Jesus" (2 Corinthians 1:20, NIV). If He did otherwise, He would negate His Son's death on the cross.

Jesus died a horrid death so that Imelda Marcos could be forgiven for her greed, so that Jeffrey Dahmer could be forgiven for his atrocities, so that Madonna could be forgiven for her wantonness, and so that Kay Rizzo could be forgiven for her self-centeredness.

My friend Sara aborted her baby 20 years ago. "I don't believe God can or will forgive me for what I've done," she admitted. No matter how hard she prayed in the passing years, she couldn't find the assurance that her sins had been forgiven.

She did not understand the significance of the shedding of the blood of Jesus Christ on the cross. She could not accept that Jesus had already suffered the ultimate punishment for all sin, including the sin that tormented her. There is no sin so terrible that cannot be completely covered by the blood of Jesus Christ.

If I say that God cannot forgive my sins, I commit an even greater sin than the one for which I wish absolution. I am saying either that my standards are higher than God's, or that Christ's sacrifice wasn't good enough to cover my misdeeds, or, even more ludicrous, that somehow I wasn't included in His promise of forgiveness. Sooner or later, either each of us must accept Jesus' death for our sins or we each will die for our sins.

It is difficult to believe that the perfect Son of God could become sin for the young mother who purposely drowned her babies, that He became sin for the hooker in east Los Angeles who will do anything for another snort of cocaine, and for the Beverly Hills madam who traffics in the flesh of starstruck young women dreaming of Hollywood fame.

On the cross Jesus cried out, "My God, my God, why have you forsaken me?" (Matthew 27:46, NIV). At that moment the God who promises "never to leave you; never to forsake you" (see Hebrews 13:5) was forced to do the unthinkable. The repulsiveness of sin forced God the Father to step back from His beloved Son in order to grant us the gift of salvation. That gift guarantees that the Father's love will never step back from you and me when we bring our sins to Him.

What great love He has for us to do such an unnatural act. Because of that love and the Son's incredible sacrifice, we are brought face-to-face with our Father each time we confess our sins. Face-to-face. We are never closer to Him than when we ask forgiveness.

In addition, our God doesn't hold grudges. I understand grudges. I come from a long line of grudge holders. My mother and my grandmother didn't speak to each other for three years, even after my parents lost their possessions in a fire or after the birth of their first grandchild. After a disagreement between my father and his brother, my uncle vowed never to speak to my dad again. He kept that promise for 20 years, until my father was on his deathbed.

God not only forgives us and offers us total cleansing from our guilt, but He plunges our sins into the deepest part of the sea. Unfortunately, over the years I've become quite proficient at deep-sea diving. Every once in a while my overactive memory dons a wet suit and fins, and hauls up from the ocean every past mistake I've made. Then I mull over my mistakes until my self-worth is devastated and I doubt that God could ever really love me. Before I finish mulling, a lifetime of sins have entangled themselves about me like spent fishing lure, threatening to drown me in self-hate.

Satan says, "Kay, you're worthless. You're nothing more than dirt." And he's half right. Whether white sand, black loam, red clay, or yellow silt, we're all just plain dirt. But praise God, the Creator chose to use dirt as the medium for designing the crowning glory of His creation. He molded Eve's gentle curves out of Eden's dust. He sculpted Adam's strong muscular physique out of simple, everyday variety dirt. And Jesus loved us so much that He died for that dirt. We are an acquisition, bought and paid for on the cross.

Again and again and again, throughout the entire Bible, the Creator says, "I love you. You're worth it all."

By kneeling in forgiveness, we acknowledge that love, we accept His sacrifice, and ask His forgiveness. At the foot of the cross we can trust Him with our deepest pain, our most repulsive sins, and our most painful memories. From there we arise to our feet praising God, confident that we've been washed totally clean. We become spiritual virgins through His grace.

This is truth—not emotional hype, but a fact upon which you and I can depend. Victory is ours through Jesus' sacrifice. And for an encore the Saviour burst from the grave and demolished the gates of hell. We will never be able to praise Him enough for that gift.

What does our praise have to do with Christ dying on the cross? Everything. The psalmist says, "Praise the Lord, O my soul, and forget not all his benefits—[for he] forgives" (Psalm 103:2, 3, NIV).

One of the definitions for praise is "confess." The passion of praise is the gift of unwarranted forgiveness. We don't deserve to be forgiven. The prayer for forgiveness and praise is the key in the hand of faith that can free us from the spiral of death.

The moment the first negative thought enters your mind is the moment to begin praising God. When you thank Him for His Son, Jesus; for the cross; and for the promise of eternal life, the destructive spiral of death never has the chance to get started.

Often Christians confuse guilt with remorse. Guilt is satanic. It drives us away from God. Remorse, on the other hand, draws us closer to Him. A way to distinguish whether the burden of past mistakes is from God or Satan is by their sheer weight. God's burden is light. When the Holy Spirit convicts our hearts of sin, He works gently, as a still small voice steadily wooing us to salvation. By contrast, Satan heaps on the guilt until the load we carry threatens to bury us.

The passion of praise is God's simple remedy for either problem. When we ask for and claim the forgiveness of our sins, and thank Him for making that forgiveness possible, we praise His holy name for being the God who forgives. When we go deep-sea diving and dig up all those rotting errors again, we show our mistrust for God's goodness.

God's second vow when we praise Him and forget not His benefits is to heal all our diseases (see verse 3, NIV). Healing? In Jesus' day, of course, but today? With our vast knowledge of medicine and nutrition, surely we don't need this stipulation, right? On the contrary, it seems that every time we turn on the television we hear of a new disease or another deadly virus for which there is no cure.

When Jesus was on this earth, living out the will of His Father, He repeatedly interchanged the phrases "Thy sins be forgiven thee" and "Be ye healed." He forgives our sins; He heals our diseases. His power is no less today than it was when the Saviour healed entire villages of their sicknesses.

At times God's healing is instantaneous. At other times it is a gradual process. Many wounds must first be cleansed in order to heal properly. This takes time.

For emotional and spiritual healing, forgiveness is the astringent that cleans our wounds of anger, resentment, and self-pity. Science has repeatedly proved that the relationship between the mind and the body is interactive. Our physical state affects our thoughts, moods, and feelings. Likewise, our thoughts, moods, and feelings affect our physical state. The healing process is inhibited by negative thinking. And the quickest way to break the habit of negative thinking is by using the key of praise. A number of years ago I experienced job burnout. Not only did our family lose a second income, but at the same time we moved to an area where the cost of living was twice as high as before. During that time Kelli grieved the death of her best friend, Rhonda almost lost her life with anorexia, and I was reduced to an invalid existence. My days were filled with futile "what ifs" and "whys," and my nights with tearful nightmares. Through all of this Richard struggled to hold down three jobs to keep us from bankruptcy. Satan schemed to destroy our family.

I don't tell you this to evoke pity. Quite the contrary. I share the story of my weakness in order to demonstrate to you how God keeps His promises. For while living with this despair, I came across Revelation 3:11: "I am coming soon.

Hold on to what you have so that no one will take your crown" (NIV).

Enough is enough, I decided. I'd allowed my enemies to rob me of too much already—my health, livelihood, family, peace, joy, and love for others. I wouldn't let them rob me of my crown as well.

When the Holy Spirit showed me that to be healed, I must first forgive my enemies, I argued, "But I have a right to be angry after what they did to me."

The words of Jesus washed through my mind: "Forgive us our debts, as we forgive our debtors."

"I can't, Lord. You're asking too much of me. I have a right to be angry! I have a right!"

"You're wrong, Kay," the Father reminded me. "You gave up the right to harbor anger and resentment when you became My daughter."

I hadn't thought of that. By choosing to become His daughter, I could no longer behave like the "heathens" do. It was a difficult idea for me to accept.

"Love is the power behind forgiveness. But it does not work the way a lot of people suppose. Love is not a soft and fuzzy sentiment that lets people get away with almost anything, no matter what they do to us. Love does not make us pushovers for people who hurt us. Love forgives, but only because love is powerful."[1]

When we as Christians harbor unresolved anger and resentment, we poison our families and our churches with our venom. Pent-up anger gets misdirected toward whoever is within shouting distance, be it the spouse, the kids, or the dog. Some of the most critical people I know are little more than angry children trying to hurt others as much as they themselves are hurting. Unforgiveness is limiting their Christian growth to a second-rate lifestyle.

The Holy Spirit was right. My enemies weren't losing sleep over what they did to me. I was. I was the one doped up on prescription medication for migraines. I was the one retreating into myself and thus driving my family further from me. I was the one toying with the idea of suicide. Something in me had to change.

The Holy Spirit led me to begin confessing to God all the resentments I could remember, and there were many. I'd been storing them for years! I confessed not only my anger at the people who hurt me, but my resentment at institutions, ways of thinking, and ways of acting. I resented some of the officials of my church, the "fat cats" in Washington, the IRS, and yes, the president of the United States. I discovered that as long I resented these people, they controlled me. J. Keith Miller in his book *Sin: Overcoming the Ultimate Deadly Addiction* recorded the words of a friend: "I am letting such people live rent-free in my head."[2]

If I wanted to be healed, I would have to allow the Holy Spirit to detoxify my brain. The poisons emitted from my resentment were killing me. As I began mechanically forgiving my enemies, I learned that forgiveness is a journey, not a destination. I didn't automatically arrive at forgiveness with my first declaration, but I did take tiny steps closer to my goal. And by the time God prepared my mind to receive the concept of praise, I was well on my way toward healing.

The authors of *The Journey Toward Wholeness* put it this way: "The body of Christ still bears the wounds of the crucifixion. Their presence is a powerful symbol of God's willingness to suffer with us. The scars also reflect an important aspect of the healing process. As we move toward wholeness, negative attitudes, emotions, and habits have less and less control over us. Depression and anxiety are replaced with joy, confidence, and trust. Our healed wounds are neither repressed nor denied. Rather they become an integrated part of the fabric of our lives."[3]

Most of the people I meet tell me, "I don't have any trouble with the forgiving; it's the forgetting that gets me." Bad memories don't automatically disappear once we forgive. We may forgive completely, but we can never forget completely. It goes against the way God made us.

The computer God placed in my brain records and stores

everything I see, hear, smell, taste, and feel. And when we forgive, the remembered event ceases to control our lives. We are no longer obsessed with it. Relinquishment is necessary to allow God to heal the injuries inflicted upon us.

In the third point of our contract with God, He promises to redeem our lives "from the pit" (Psalm 103:4, NIV). For me, that pit was the well of depression. Slime and moss covered the walls of my pit. No matter how often I clawed partway up the sides of my pit, I would, sooner or later, slide back to the bottom with the decomposing corpses of my past. I learned that the well of depression contains three nots:

1. *Not trusting Jesus.* I wanted everything done now and in my way, not His. Rebellion is the pivotal point on which all ugly behavioral patterns turn: self-pity, anger, resentment, hardness of heart, self-centeredness. The spirit of rebellion shuts the door in God's face. We are saying, "You failed me, God. I'll do it my way now. I'll be the boss of my life!"

2. *Not valuing His grace.* Conditioning makes us fall into the trap of believing that how much God loves us is in direct relation to our behavior. In turn, when we relate that same principle to other people, they let us down, and we become depressed. It's only as we recognize the value of God's grace that we can grant His grace to other people.

3. *Not abiding in His kindness,* the simple homespun kindness of Jesus' love. He says, "Be content with what you have, because God has said, 'Never will I leave you; never will I forsake you'" (Hebrews 13:5, NIV).

Daily, as I praise Him, He fulfills His pledge to "[crown me] with love and compassion" (Psalm 103:4, NIV). Talk about love and compassion! I find it in the strangest of places.

I was stranded at a small airport for several hours because of bad weather conditions. A short time before my scheduled takeoff, I realized I hadn't eaten anything since breakfast. And I knew that my two-hour flight would be made in a plane that had no food or water facilities.

Since there were no restaurants open, I wandered over to the concession machines, chose a pack of crackers and peanut butter, opened my wallet, and discovered that I had no change and no bills smaller than $10. I asked the ticket agent if she had change. She shook her head. I looked around at the other waiting passengers. I am not an aggressive person when it comes to facing off with a stranger. But I knew that if I didn't eat something soon, my sugar level would drop dangerously low before I reached my final destination.

Hiding my reluctance behind a smile, I approached a middle-aged man reading a newspaper. "Sir, do you have change for a $10?" I asked.

Without looking up from his paper, he shook his head. After such an out-of-hand rejection, I was doubly fearful of asking again. I waited a few minutes, then chose another gentleman. This man rattled off what I believed to be a no in another language.

I started to walk back to my seat when a woman who'd been watching me called, "I have some quarters." Reaching into her purse for her wallet, she poured a handful of coins into my hands.

"Here, let me give you my $10."

She shook her head and smiled. "No—"

Tears sprang into my eyes. "But I can't just let you give them to me."

She grinned again. "I'm not giving them to you. All I'm doing is passing on to you a kindness I've received. When you get a chance, you do the same."

I never imagined I'd have the opportunity to fulfill my benefactor's commission so soon. Late that evening while I waited for my car and driver to come for me, a young mother with two toddlers clinging to her legs asked me if I had change for a dollar. The shops were all closed, the change machines broken, and she'd lost what coins she had in a malfunctioning telephone. "My husband will be worried sick. My plane was three hours late."

I didn't take her dollar bill. Instead, as I told her my story, I took out my wallet and dumped the change into her hand. "Now, you pass it on, OK?"

She gave me a quick hug, scooped up her babies, and ran to find a telephone that worked.

Yes, He fills my life with love and compassion.

The psalmist told us that God enjoys satisfying our "desires with good things" (Psalm 103:5, NIV). Living in the central valley of California, I am teased about "living in the land of fruits and nuts." I readily agree. I've never lived in a place in which there were more good things to eat. Talk about abundance! A few minutes ago I scooped out and ate the last triangle of meat from a sweet, juicy grapefruit. In the middle of my dining room table I keep a three-tiered pie server filled with California's best—all year round. I can't peel a tangerine without praising God. I can't pop a pistachio nut without remembering His goodness.

As I enjoy God's abundant blessings, "[my] youth is [being] renewed like the eagle's" (verse 5, NIV). I tell everyone who will listen that the 45-year-old woman who couldn't walk from the parking lot to the United Airlines flight gate in the airport terminal without resting several times now has the energy of a 25-year-old. Praise God for His healing power! Now, if only I could figure out where that 25-year-old keeps her body!

---

[1] Lewis Smedes, *Forgive and Forget: Healing the Hurts We Don't Deserve* (New York: Pocket Books, 1984), p. 182.

[2] J. Keith Miller, *Sin: Overcoming the Ultimate Deadly Addiction* (San Francisco: Harper and Row Publishers, 1987), p. 142.

[3] K. L. Bakken and K. H. Hoffeller, *The Journey Toward Wholeness*, p. 66.

CHAPTER NINE

Healing and Praise

Whatever poet penned the words "O Lord, I thank You for this amazing day" must have been sitting on my shoulder this morning as I enjoyed the beauty of sunlight streaming through my office windows. I threw open my windows and patio doors and inhaled the fresh, clean air. The balmy springtime breeze got busy chasing winter's stagnant air out of the crannies and nooks of my home. Another central California winter has passed, and the triple-digit temperatures of summer are still several months away.

Corky, my 10-year-old Sheltie, and Meow—her name is self-explanatory—are taking advantage of their freedom to wander in and out of the house at will. What a joy it is to be alive today. I feel like singing, dancing, laughing.

"I can feel Your presence, Lord, as I write these words. You have brought me through another cold, foggy winter where except for Your continued presence I might have lost my way. But You were there for me just as You promised— every step of the way."

The winters in central California are mild compared to the winters my husband and I endured living in upstate New York and in Wisconsin. Now, those were winters! Yet California midwinter blahs can be equally devastating. A poster taped to the ceiling of my dentist's examination room recently caught my attention. "In a way, winter is the real spring, the time when inner things happen—the resurge of nature."[1]

During my months of spiritual winter, inner things were happening but I didn't know that God was leading me through the steps of healing. First, I needed to spend time with my Saviour, time beyond a quick "read" and prayer. I had to learn firsthand how good God really is. I needed to crave His presence like the deer described in Psalm 42 pants for cool, fresh water.

I continued my daily regimen of walking my way to better health. However, I added a new twist that doubled the benefits. I made my physical exercise a time of praise and prayer. Walking the first block, I praised God in song and scripture—sometimes in full voice, other times in whispers. During the second block I prayed for myself, inviting the Holy Spirit to fill me completely. While I walked the next block I lifted Richard to God in praise; the fourth block, Rhonda; then Kelli; and so forth. Each person on my prayer list had his or her own block of praise. This was not a time for dredging up each person's problems as I perceived them to be, but a time for rejoicing in that person and in God's love for him or her. And no matter how gloomy my day was before I left the house, by the time I returned home the sun would be shining, at least in my heart.

My next step was to admit I had a problem. This isn't as easy as it sounds. Ask any practicing psychologist.

"I'm not guilty of pride. I've been hurt."

"I'm not being petty. I've been wounded."

"I'm not unforgiving. I was an abused child."

"My fear isn't from a lack of faith. I'm having an anxiety attack."

"My lack of joy isn't a sin. I'm depressed."

One day a woman, cursed for 12 years with uncontrollable bleeding, touched the edge of Jesus' robe and was instantly healed. When Jesus asked, "Who touched Me?" the disciples laughed. His question seemed ridiculous, considering the crowd that pushed and crowded around them. However, Christ's question wasn't for His edification, but to facilitate the steps necessary for her emotional healing.

She'd been an outcast from society for 12 years. Besides her physical problems, she bore the emotional wounds of fear, guilt, and resentment. For the woman to be wholly healed, these wounds had to be opened to allow the cleansing of her heart and soul, just as her sick body had been healed.

Similar to this dear woman, I needed to put my past in the past for me to become whole again. I had to forgive myself for not living up to my own unrealistic expectations. Then I had to forgive God for the disappointment I felt when I discovered that He didn't fit into the little box I'd created for Him. He didn't play by my rules. He didn't play any games at all. My little religious games ran amok whenever I came face-to-face with His simple command—"Love one another as I have loved you." I wasn't sure I liked that.

My healing couldn't happen until I learned to forgive family members for injuries real or imagined, to forgive friends for slights intended or otherwise. Forgiveness wasn't so much for their benefit, but for mine. *I* needed the healing. I had to let go of my pain.

This was difficult. As much as I knew I had to do it, I still fought it. I argued with God and myself. *How can I ever forgive those people who set out to destroy me and my family?* Yet I knew that Christ's model prayer, "Forgive us our debts, as we forgive our debtors," wasn't a mere suggestion. It's the way the law of forgiveness works. I could be forgiven only to the extent I forgive.

"But you don't know what I've been through," some say.

"No, I don't, but Jesus does."

"I had a bad childhood. You can't imagine how bad!"

"Probably not, but neither can you begin to understand how good God is."

"Have you ever been raped?"

"No, but Christ suffered your humiliation. He hung naked on the cross for all the world to gape at and ridicule."

"Has your husband ever betrayed you with another woman?"

"No, but again, Jesus understands the pain of betrayal, and He feels the tears of the abused." I've had troubles. We all have.

And while we might not share the same trial, we all feel the resulting pain.

Every command God gives contains three benefits. When He commands us to forgive others as we are forgiven, we are assured of:

1. Protection. By forgiving those who hurt us, our obedience protects us against unnecessary stress, stress-related illnesses, depression, burnout, and possibly suicide—to name a few.

2. Promise. By forgiving, we will, in turn, be forgiven. God promises to heal the brokenhearted and set the prisoner free (Isaiah 61:1).

3. Provision. There is no pain so excruciating as an injury to the soul. There is no prison so confining as the darkness of despair. And God's provision for our release is forgiveness.

~

I started with those closest to me and worked outward. I never imagined how far God wanted me to go in this business of forgiveness. Let me tell you a story.

During the Japanese occupation of Korea during World War II, public assembly of the nationals was curtailed, including religious meetings. The military ordered that the churches be closed. When a group of Christians wanted to meet for one last service they applied for and received the necessary permission. The day of the scheduled meeting the church was packed with worshipers. While the people inside sang "At the Cross," Japanese soldiers barricaded the exits, then set fire to the building. All the worshipers were killed.

The fire died to ashes, but flames of hatred burned within the hearts of other Korean Christians. When Japan withdrew their forces at the end of the war, the Koreans built a memorial to the slain Christians on the very spot the church once stood. This memorial only reminded them of the disaster.

In 1971 a group of Japanese tourists traveling through Korea chanced upon the monument. When they read the names of the people killed there and learned the story, they were overcome with shame. They returned to Japan and raised 10 million yen ($25,000) to erect a new church on the site of the tragedy.

They sent a delegation to the dedication service. Speeches were made, the tragedy was recalled, and the dead honored, yet the hate that had festered for decades could still be felt within the sanctuary. At the end of the service the congregation stood to sing the closing hymn, "At the Cross," and something remarkable happened.

Tears flowed from the eyes of the usually composed Japanese. They turned to their spiritual relatives and begged for forgiveness. The hate-filled hearts of the Koreans broke as they sang the chorus: "At the cross, at the cross where I first saw the light, and the burden of my heart rolled away." The floodgates of emotion could no longer be held back. Tears of repentance and forgiveness bathed the wounds of bitterness and hatred, leaving only reconciliation and love in their place.

A few years after hearing this story, I was a guest speaker at a women's retreat. I'd been talking about forgiveness found at the cross of Jesus Christ, and I felt impressed to do something I'd never done before. I could hardly believe what I heard myself saying.

"Tonight I come to you from a long line of rogues and rapists, murderers and marauders, thieves and scoundrels. My ancestors, in an effort to secure for themselves and their children a new home in a new land, stole the land from others and drove them far from their homes. My 'blue-blooded' predecessors made their fortunes on the backs of slave labor. They seared the brand of hatred indelibly into the hearts and minds of generations that would follow. For hate begets hate. Fear begets fear.

"On the night before He died, my beautiful Saviour said, 'I pray also for those [you and me] who will believe in me through their [the disciples] message, that all . . . may be one, Father, just as you are in me and I am in you' [John

17:20, 21, NIV]. I look around, and I don't see that happening, my sisters.

"Our cities stagger from blood spewing from the gaping wounds of resentment. In our churches we wear masks of civility, but just beneath the surface, hostility seethes and burns unstopped. We cluster together, likes with likes, afraid that if we reach out to one another we will be rebuffed. Or worse yet, we are afraid we might have to let go of that little snippet of pride or that shred of treasured heritage we've clung to all our lives. My Saviour prayed that we would become one.

"Jeremiah the prophet prayed, 'We acknowledge, O Lord, our wickedness, and the iniquity of our fathers' (Jeremiah 14:20).

"Nehemiah tells how the Israelites stood before God and 'confessed their sins and the wickedness of their fathers' (Nehemiah 9:2, NIV).

"And so I come to you tonight, humbly asking your forgiveness for the sins of my predecessors, the sins that still burn hot in your souls, the treachery that never seems to stop. Please forgive me if I've ever hurt you. I stand in the place of my ancestors, asking you to forgive the sins they committed against your fathers and mothers, and brothers and sisters.

"The healing of the nations can begin right here, tonight."

All the while I spoke I prayed silently, *Lord, are You sure You want me to do this?* I had no idea how my audacious request for forgiveness would be taken by my White sisters. Would they bristle at the idea of my begging forgiveness for the sins of their race? I wondered how my Asian sisters would accept what I said. They too suffered at the hands of Caucasians. And certainly not the least, I worried how my African-American sisters would react. Would they think me naive, or flippant with such a serious problem? Would they question my sincerity? Worse yet, would they think I did it all for effect, for good theatrics? I had no idea. I just knew the Holy Spirit wanted me to do it, and I had no choice.

The story didn't end until the next evening in the ladies'

room. One of my African-American sisters told me, "Last night a group of 'sisters' stayed up 'till all hours of the night talking about what you said."

I held my breath, preparing myself for the worst.

"And I was elected to tell you that we accept your apology. We too want to facilitate the oneness of Jesus." Our eyes filled with tears as we tentatively reached out to one another. What an incredible gift she and her "sisters" gave me, one I will always treasure.

"Forgiveness brings change. When we accept God's forgiveness we relinquish personal judgments about ourselves and others. We must lose our sense of identity as defined by old attitudes, feeling, needs and accept our new foreign selves."[2]

By relinquishing my pride in my "blue blood," I received a transfusion of the royal blood of Jesus Christ. Such a sacrifice! Nonsense! The only sacrifice in sight was the one Jesus gave on Calvary.

---

[1] Edna O'Brien.
[2] K. L. Bakken and K. H. Hoffeller, *The Journey Toward Wholeness*, p. 74.

CHAPTER TEN

Moving On

The moving on part—this is where it gets exciting. This is where God promises to take my weaknesses, my most shameful memories, and turn them into my greatest strengths. Can you imagine being able to praise God and bring glory to His name through your ugliest weakness! I couldn't, but it's true.

I don't know about you, but I've got an enormous list of "weaknesses and shames" from which to choose. And when I've finished here, some of you may wish I'd chosen to reveal one of the others instead. However, if I had to choose one shame that bothers me above all others, I would have to say it's my weight.

From my conversations with women of all sizes, shapes, and cultures, I know that I'm far from alone fighting my obsession with weight loss. This reality hit me when a five-foot-six-inch, 105-pound strikingly beautiful female friend of mine tearfully admitted that hardly an hour goes by without her becoming anxious about her weight. Cindy told me she has three wardrobes—her "skinny" clothes for days when she feels good about herself (these are the least worn); her "normal" days' clothing; and clothes to wear on her "fat" days, when she must conceal the ugly bulges only she sees whenever she looks in a mirror. I laughed.

"Honey, you saying that you have fat days is like a bald woman complaining of having a bad hair day!"

She laughed along, but Cindy's anxiety was real. She

explained that her entire identity is wrapped up in her perceptions about her body. Anxiety and fear plague her every hour of the day. She admits that "food is my master. I never stop thinking about either what I just ate or will eat, what I can eat or can't eat." Her faith in God's loving acceptance of her rises and falls with the needle on her bathroom scale.

Millions of American women obsess over their weight. As for me, I've had a weight problem since my pediatrician put me on my first low-fat diet at 6 months of age. Since then, I've done them all—cottage cheese, pineapple, brewer's yeast, prescription diet pills, diet candy, water, and what can only be described as liquid chalk. One doctor, thinking to encourage me after a particularly good week of dieting, told me about a favorite uncle of his—or at least he would have been the doctor's favorite uncle, except for his obesity. "I couldn't stand to have the man put his fat arms around me," the doctor admitted.

I went home, my determination intensified by my fear of rejection. I ran. I jogged. I did calisthenics. I swam. And I assure you, I lost weight. Every diet worked. I lost hundreds of pounds! Unfortunately, each time I reached my goal weight, the pounds returned with a vengeance. With the last three diets I almost lost my life as well. That's when the Holy Spirit opened my eyes to my problem.

My god wasn't the God of creation. Like Cindy, I worshiped at the altar of food. Unlike Cindy, I ate the food instead of obsessing over it. And when my worst fears became reality, I turned to Mrs. See for solace rather than the Comforter. I sought for leftovers in the refrigerator instead of seeking first the kingdom of God.

As I learned about the power of praise, I took on the monster of obesity. One way or another, I would give thanks! I pounded out my chant across the darkened playing field. "I'm glad I'm fat! I'm glad I'm fat! I'm lying, Lord. I'm lying, Lord! I can never be grateful for being overweight! How can You ask me to be?" I knew the problem was my fault, not His, and I hated myself for it.

Three years later I am still overweight. Does that mean God isn't answering my prayer of healing? Does it mean His arm is too short to meet my needs? No, absolutely not. My healing had to begin from within before He and I could make the necessary lasting external changes. I needed to let Him heal the scars that caused the weight gain before tackling my surface problem. That fact does not excuse me from submitting to His guidelines for maintaining a healthy diet, a regular exercise plan, and a merry heart. In all things, I must let Him lead.

I needed to forgive myself for my weaknesses. I had to forgive God for not performing a quick fix to my weight problem. I needed to be transformed by the renewing of my mind before my body could respond. I needed to "take captive every thought to make it obedient to Christ" (2 Corinthians 10:5, NIV) and to set my mind "on things above" (Colossians 3:2, NIV).

This isn't so easy. Scars inflicted in childhood had to be uncovered. My memories had to be cleansed of festering resentment and exposed to the pure sunlight of God's love. Praise God, this process is still going on within me.

The first evidence I had that my healing had begun was when I discovered that after I survived a major personal crisis, I didn't gain weight. For years, with every family crisis I put on 20 additional pounds within a month's time, and the pounds stayed. This time I didn't. Instead, I lost five pounds. Nothing else in my life had changed, nothing except my choice to praise instead of complain.

One day I was walking across the grounds of a camp meeting at which I was a guest speaker. A determined woman saw me and strode up to me, shaking her bony finger in my face. "Do you know that you are fat?" she asked.

I looked at her in surprise, then down at my body, first from one angle, then another before replying, "Well, would you look at that! You're right. I am fat. Thank you so much for telling me."

Her mouth fell open in surprise. Before I could slip

away, she regained her composure and resumed her mission. "Do you know that there will be no fat people in heaven?"

"Who do you think you are?" the old Kay wanted to shout in her face. The new Kay prayed for grace. "Why, you're right again, sister. Praise God, there won't be any fat people in heaven. And you know what else? There won't be any proud people, or critical people, or hurtful people there either." I smiled. "Isn't it wonderful the changes God can make in each of us if we just let Him?"

She dropped her gaze, mumbled about having another appointment, and hurried away. As for me, I wanted to sing. I wanted to dance. I wanted to shout "Hallelujah." My response was evidence to me that my Father was in the process of healing me. Previously a look, a word, or even a gesture about my weight problem could send me to bed in tears.

Lest you think this little story is a rare case, let me tell you about a saintly but overweight pastor who was accosted by one of his parishioners. "How can you stand in the pulpit and preach the gospel of Jesus Christ, looking like you do?" the pastor was asked.

The mother-in-law of a young friend of mine—a friend who is far from obese—is driving steel stakes between herself and her son's wife by constantly pointing out how well she, the mother-in-law, maintains her weight. The woman eats large, high-cholesterol meals that always include a luscious decadent dessert, all the while advising her daughter-in-law not to eat so much. The woman has never weighed more than 125 pounds in her entire 52 years. If her criticism continues, this woman will lose the love of not only her son's wife, but the affection of her son as well.

Often in our effort to preach the benefits of a healthy diet as a way of life, we fasten it to God's acceptance of us, like a slice of melted cheese on a Veggie burger. They don't go together. It's not that obese people don't know they have a problem. Of course they know. They're reminded by every mirror, by every plate-glass window, by every piece of clothing into which they squeeze.

When I paced the playing field in the night, thanking God for my obesity, I never guessed how He could turn my shame into genuine gratitude. Today, while I make the necessary adjustments in my lifestyle to facilitate the shedding of excess poundage, while the Holy Spirit is still uncovering scars that need healing, I can honestly give thanks. I can be confident that God's power is made perfect in my weakness and in my shame (2 Corinthians. 12:9, 10).

It isn't easy to speak before hundreds of women about the most sensitive aspect of my life. I can hardly talk with my husband about my problem.

"Then why do you do it?" some women ask. My answer is found in the same text. Here Paul gives one of the most promising messages in the Word of God. "Therefore I will boast all the more gladly about my weaknesses, so that Christ's power may rest on me. . . . I delight in weaknesses, in insults, in hardships, in persecutions, in difficulties. For when I am weak, then I am strong."

Jesus became vulnerable for me so that I could become victorious for Him. Nails didn't hold my Saviour to the cross; His love held Him there. The Romans didn't take His life; He gave it willingly. He broke the chains of death so that I might walk free and in good health. What a loving, healing Jesus.

God is using my healing time to bring glory to His name. I'd still like for my body to be sleek and firm one day, but until I reach that goal, He has given me a new ministry, one of joy which I can share with my overweight sisters. Quite honestly, if I waited until I was slim to tell my story, many wouldn't listen to what I had to say.

Almost every time I speak on this subject, women come up to me afterward and say, "I am so glad that you aren't a Barbie Doll type trying to tell us poor mortals how to live. Thank you for being so real."

God is allowing me to share a ministry of promise for my Barbie Doll-perfect sisters, and those not quite perfect ones as well. Even those with "perfect" figures have weaknesses too. As I share my experience in honestly facing my problem, they can learn how to deal with their most hidden shame too.

It is a fact, not a fancy, that God will glorify Himself through us by turning our most hated weaknesses into our greatest strengths. By His power He will transform our most despicable shame into incredible joy if we let Him. And it's no surprise that reaching out to meet others' needs is part of God's plan of recovery. Who can better understand and assist a rape victim than someone who's experienced the degradation of rape? Who can better help an alcoholic to break the cycle of alcoholism than a recovering alcoholic? Who can better share the freedom found in the amazing grace of Jesus Christ than a former slave trader?

In Christ Jesus the obese woman can "boast of the things [pounds] that show [her] weakness" (2 Corinthians 11:30, NIV), for in doing so, she can glorify God and give Him all her praise.

Perhaps weight is not your problem. You might be one of those fortunate little butterflies whose digestive system seems to be lined with Teflon. *Your* weakness, your greatest shame, might not be so evident to public scrutiny as mine, but I promise you, the key to overcoming is the same. No healing and no forgiveness can happen by any other vehicle than the cross of Jesus Christ. And the golden bridge that gets us there is praise and thanksgiving.

CHAPTER ELEVEN

Claiming My Inheritance

I come from a long line of fighting rebels—George Washington, John Hancock, and James Madison during early America, and General W. S. Hancock during the Civil War—or so family genealogists have reported. In the process of spotting famous and not-so-famous ancestors, these energetic researchers have uncovered several interesting tales. While I've not personally researched the following family legend, I've been told that it is true.

Two Sherwood brothers came to America from England before the Revolutionary War. When the fighting broke out between the English and the Colonists, they sided with the rebels. For their faithful service, the Sherwood boys each received a land grant in western Pennsylvania from their commander-in-chief, George Washington.

Unfortunately the tribes of Native Americans previously living on the acreage sided with the English and were forced to vacate. Years passed, along with several generations of Sherwoods.

The story goes that one day a finely dressed English barrister arrived on the doorstep of a distant great-grandfather of mine. The lawyer announced that the last in a line of Sherwoods had died, leaving his estate and his title to the male heir next in line—my great-grandfather.

"The only requirement," the attorney explained confidently, "is that you become an English citizen and reside on the family estate for at least 10 years."

The old man curled his lip (so legend tells it) and replied, "Sir, you might as well pack up your bags and head home. England ain't never done nothin' for me. I'm right happy where I am." The price was too high.

Whether or not the story is true is immaterial now, so many generations later. Yet in a moment of fancy, I can't help wondering how different my life would have been as a wealthy heir. That's before I remember that I *am* an heir. I have a delightful inheritance. "The Lord assigned me my portion and my cup. He made my lot secure. And the boundary lines have fallen for me in pleasant places" (see Psalm 16:5, 6).

Our portion, our position in the family of God, was secured by Christ's blood. Our cup (Psalm 23:5; 116:13) is the blessings we receive as family members.

When the leaders in ancient Israel divided up the land afforded to each tribe and family, the lots were secured by law. Some of the lots were better than others. While some lots might have fallen on rocky, unproductive soil, others fell on rich loam. Our lot in the kingdom of God, our inheritance, is also secure and the boundaries of our place are pleasant. Our heritage is delightful.

Unfortunately, for many years I worked so hard to fill what I thought were my family obligations and responsibilities, I didn't take the time to learn how to effectively draw on my inheritance.

It is true. We do have obligations. Father God wants us to wear the family name with pride. That's an obligation, but it's also a privilege. A few years ago William Kennedy Smith learned during his rape trial in Palm Beach how valuable his Kennedy name was.

At the first hint of trouble, he hoofed it north to the Hyannis Port compound to get help. Grandma Rose could have said, "Too bad, sonny! You blew it. Don't come crying to me." But she didn't. Instead she put all the family resources at his disposal, including the best Boston lawyers and Hollywood acting coaches.

Young Billy could have told his grandmother, "I know what I'm doing. Mind your own business. I can do this myself." But if nothing else, the Kennedy puppy wasn't a fool. He knew he was a Kennedy—for better or worse. His place in the family was secure. Would the same assistance have been granted one of the Kennedy servants? Probably not. "A [servant] has no permanent place in the family, but [a son or daughter] belongs to it forever" (John 8:35, NIV).

As children of God another family obligation we have is to spend time with Him. He wants us to get to know Him better. He speaks to us through the Holy Spirit and His Word. By choosing to praise Him, we live continually in the presence of God. And by choosing to live continually in His presence, the mind of Christ can be in us (1 Corinthians 2:16). That's incredible! Think about it.

The mind bequeathed to us by sin is death, but the mind controlled by the Spirit is life. That's a definite privilege. And not Christ's mind only but His character will be perfectly reproduced within us—all made possible by living in the Spirit and the Spirit living in us.

All of us were born with family traits and abilities. Some appear at birth. I inherited my mother's ears—they tip out at the top like a pixie's. I did nothing to earn them; they are mine as my mother's daughter. Other family traits appeared later, as I grew: freckles, a spitfire temper, my quirky sense of humor, and my interest in writing and music. Some came as the results of hereditary factors, and others, environment.

I always enjoy watching a little boy ape his father's swagger. As the child grows older he won't even be conscious of how much he's like his dad. It's in his genes. It's his right to be like his dad.

Most likely, the code of ethics by which the father lives will sooner or later be adopted by the son. The boy will see that his father's conduct is controlled by his code of ethics. His personality will reflect that code. For instance, if the father believes that a gentleman always treats women with respect, he will be polite and considerate to all the women he meets. The son will observe his father's courtesy over time, and he will probably treat women with the same respect.

Whether we call it growing in Jesus, walking in the Spirit, living in a Spirit of abundance, or living in the kingdom of God, it is our birthright to become like our Dad. We wear Designer genes. And we develop the character of God by precept and example. He teaches us in His Word, where we can see the example of His character lived out through the life of our Elder Brother, Jesus.

In addition, we have the right to ask God to develop His traits of character in our lives—the "fruit of the Spirit" (Galatians 5:22). They're not some kind of exercise practiced and practiced and practiced again until we get it right, but a natural result of growing in the Spirit. Not gifts, but *rights*. The gifts of the Spirit are distributed as God sees fit. But the fruit of the Spirit is a natural result of maturing in Christ.

I bought and potted a lemon tree a couple years ago. After two years of proper care and feeding, my little tree produced six of the best-tasting lemons found in the Central Valley—at least that's the opinion of a first-time lemon grower. I'd call *Guinness Book of Records* if next spring I found oranges or apricots instead of lemons growing on the tree's spindly branches. It's in my tree's genes to produce lemons, not apricots.

Producing the fruit of the Spirit is in our genes. If we expect to ask boldly for what is rightfully ours, it's important that we know what to ask for. While in Philippians 1:11 Paul calls them the fruit of righteousness; in Galatians he lists them. Here are some:

1. Love—We choose to love because God is love. Even if we allowed ourselves to be martyred for God, if it wasn't done in love, it's useless (1 Corinthians 13). Love is the most difficult concept to understand. A mother loves her bald,

stinky, toothless baby. A man tenderly cares for his dying wife of 60 years, caring for her in ways that would repulse him were it not for love.

2. Joy—The literal translation means "well-minded." I like that. Someone once said, "Maintain your joy and confuse the devil." James says, "Count it all joy . . ."

3. Goodness—This is a condition that is rooted in one's innermost being but is expressed in deeds. Goodness never wishes evil on anyone. As the kids say, this is "walking the walk."

4. Peace—To be at peace is a harmony between God and humanity, a shalom. Isaiah calls it "perfect."

5. Patience—Ouch! Patience isn't gritting one's teeth and counting to 10. It's a state of mind that doesn't succumb to circumstances. Patience perfects character. It grows only in trial (James 1:3).

6. Temperance—Its Greek root word *egkrateia* means "strength or power bestowed by God on human beings" (Acts 24:25). This God-control is not to be confused with the Greek word *egkrateuo-mai,* used in 1 Corinthians 9:25 and meaning the rigid self-control practiced by an athlete. This is Holy Ghost power that is ours for the asking, not a brutal self-flagellation in order to earn a gold medal at the Olympics.

7. Meekness—The word "meek" in English suggests weakness. The root word describes a condition of the heart and mind more like "gentleness." When the Lord manifested meekness, it was from a position of power because He had infinite heavenly resources at His command.[1]

Through the power of the Holy Spirit we can choose to come boldly to the throne of God at any time and request our rightful inheritance. When confronted by hate, we can choose to love. We can request a wellspring of joy to replace the cesspool of depression in our souls. We can choose to wait patiently on the Lord and refuse to be anxious.

In *Life at Its Best* Ellen White says, "Resist melancholy, discontented thoughts and feelings. . . . How can we go [to heaven] as a band of mourners, groaning and complaining all along the way to our Father's house?" Earlier on the same page she tells us that "nothing promotes health of body and of soul than does a spirit of gratitude and praise."[2]

"Lord, I need patience, and I need it now!"

This is where praise comes into its own, where living in the Spirit of abundance thrives. When I praise God, I take my attention off earthly things [my problem] and focus it on the Problem Solver. "Set your minds on things above, not on earthly things" (Colossians 3:2, NIV).

I am a born worrier. I worry about the weather, my family, my health, finances, the condition of the country, the uneaten bananas in the fruit bowl. And the list goes on. But wait, let me take you through a typical worry sequence.

I look at the clock. *H'mm, Richard's late getting home from work. He should have been here a half hour ago. I wonder what's keeping him?* I pace to the telephone, pick up the receiver, and listen. The telephone is working. My worry sequence has begun.

Maybe he had a committee meeting or something. No, he would have called. He knows how I worry. My peace has definitely been disrupted. *I wonder if he's had car trouble. I've been hearing a little ping in the engine lately. He could be stranded beside the road.*

My heart pounds as I picture those overloaded triple-trailer trucks zooming by him on the interstate. I pace to the door and look outside. No sign of him. Then a new thought occurs. *Maybe he's been in an accident. He could be hurt or, worse yet, dead!* Agitated, I glance at the clock again. Fifteen minutes pass. *What should I do, call the highway patrol, or the hospital's emergency room? Oh, dear God, please don't let anything happen to him!*

The distance is short from this prayer of desperation to my next thought. *If something happened to him, what would I do?* First, I imagine myself driving to the morgue to claim his body, then calling the family with the tragic news. Before an entire hour passes and he walks through the door with a very logical explanation for his tardiness, I have him buried, our belongings sold, and my bleak future outlined in detail.

I call this thinking process my death spiral. Within a few minutes I begin with one negative thought and spiral down into absolute depression. This despondency can color my attitude for days afterward. The same thing happens with anger, resentment, self-pity, self-disgust—you name it. My stress soars as my depression deepens. And all that peace and joy and love the Holy Spirit has been growing inside of me is temporarily frozen out.

However, I have discovered that every time I choose to praise, my attitude improves by weakening the spirit of scarcity within me and strengthening the Spirit of abundance. I am forming a habit of praising. When I begin praising on my first negative thought, it isn't so difficult to spiral back to good mental health.

"Let us educate our hearts and lips to speak the praise of God for His matchless love. . . . Never should we forget that we are children of the heavenly King, sons and daughters of the Lord of hosts."[3]

Developing a habit of praising, or living in the Spirit of abundance, has produced an interesting by-product in my life—praising has become second nature. And the moment a negative thought enters my mind I am conscious of the choice I have—to sin or not to sin. Before I learned about this, I wouldn't recognize the sin process until I was swamped with guilt and frustration. Now it's like the Holy Spirit removed my blinders and I can see my fate before I take that first step downward. Now I get to choose to be more than a conqueror—not by my power, but the Holy Spirit's (Romans 8:37).

"So, have you reached a state of perfection yet?" some might jokingly ask.

Are you kidding? Over the years I've developed enough bad spirals to last a lifetime of retraining. And while I've tasted victory over a few of my peskier sins, sometimes I knowingly choose to sin. There is a perverse pleasure, perhaps because of some negative endorphins given off by the brain, in letting one's imagination visualize the worst. But knowing where those thoughts will take me has lessened their appeal.

When I started studying into praise and living in the Spirit of abundance, I couldn't have imagined how explosive those two interlinking concepts could be. I couldn't perceive the changes that would take place in me. The joy I've experienced has soared far into the realm of the hyperbole. Prayer combined with praise has changed not only my life and my husband's life, but our marriage and our home as well. And it has spread to other family members and far beyond.

I shared my discoveries at a recent women's retreat. To accommodate the large number of attendees, the conference was held over two weekends. I'd settled in my room for the second weekend and was heading toward the main auditorium when I heard two women call my name. They ran across the parking lot shouting, "Kay, Kay, it works! It works! We tried it this week and it works!"

These two sophisticated young women grabbed me, hugged me, and whirled me about. Our tears and laughter mingled as they shouted again and again, "It works. I didn't believe it would, but I tried it and it does!"

It really does, I promise you. No, I take that back. It works, not because I say so, but because God says so. God cannot lie. If He did, He would no longer be God. That's where our confidence belongs! The Holy Spirit works on the wings of our praise to carry out the will of God in our lives.

---

[1] *Vine's Expository Dictionary,* pp. 256, 257.
[2] E. G. White, *Life at Its Best,* p. 156.
[3] *Vine's Expository Dictionary.*

CHAPTER TWELVE

The Bold and the Beautiful

C ome boldly unto the throne of grace" (Hebrews 4:16).

For the mothers in my childhood neighborhood, to be "bold" was a bad thing. Index finger wagging, one or another would command, "Don't be so bold!"

But God uses it as a positive behavior trait. In the New International Version of the Bible "bold" is translated as "confident." This confidence grace is not self-confidence, but God-confidence, not arrogance or trumped-up courage, but assuredness that one is accepted and loved. I like that.

During the Kennedy administration a prizewinning photograph was taken of Caroline Kennedy and one of her friends playing dolls beneath the lip of her father's desk in the Oval Office of the White House. Now, that's confidence. Grown men have trembled, stuttered, and shuffled nervous feet whenever they've approached the desk of the most powerful individual on the planet, but Caroline knew that she didn't need to be afraid. This was her daddy's desk, and she was his darling daughter. She could come into the presence of her father with confidence — not confidence in herself, but in him. Is it so hard to imagine that I might have that same confidence as a child of God?

God's promises are more secure than the gold ingots stored at Fort Knox, Kentucky (Psalm 119:140). They have been thoroughly tested by great women like Eve, Sarah, Naomi, Mary, Dorcas, and Priscilla.

Claiming the promises of God is like carrying a Master Charge platinum credit card. No, it goes beyond a credit card. When we become Christians we are given a checkbook on an unlimited account. It takes faith to believe that there's "money" in the bank to write a check. How tragic for the person of little faith who lives and dies without writing one check, to be a spiritual billionaire and die a spiritual pauper!

King Solomon, Queen Esther, Ruth, Rahab, Rebekah — those who lived before Jesus' death used a credit card of promises. But once God's promise was fulfilled at the cross, those of us living after, from Mary, the former prostitute, to Katharina Luther, to Mother Teresa and to me, we have a guaranteed checking account. God's promises are money in the bank. And every one of them are "Yes, in Christ," not because of anything we do, but because of what the Saviour did for us. Validated at the cross, this checkbook can be used anywhere, anytime, and it's never overdrawn!

"Wait a minute," I hear some of you saying right now. "Don't tell me that my prayers are all 'Yes' in Jesus. I've prayed many times and not had my prayers answered."

"Yes" is not my word, but the apostle Paul's in 2 Corinthians 1:20. And I too have experienced times when it seemed that God did not answer my prayers, at least not in the way I expected.

When I was young, my father lost his job for "finding religion." He decided to go into business for himself. Those who have started their own business know how difficult those first few years can be. As a result, our family went through our own "Great Depression."

I remember kneeling beside my bed and praying that God would send someone to our door with a check for $1 million to solve my daddy's problems. I'd seen the popular TV program *The Millionaire*. I'd heard my parents worrying over the family finances. And I responded as I'd been taught to respond.

Did God answer my prayer for $1 million? In a way, yes.

I admit that no $1 million check showed up in my father's bank account. But God knew the true desires of His little daughter's heart. He knew that I had no idea how much money $1 million really was (and I still don't!). He knew what I really wanted wasn't cash, but security. I wanted my safe little world restored.

Centuries earlier the psalmist wrote: "I have never seen the righteous forsaken or their children begging bread" (Psalm 37:25, NIV). God answered my prayer, not by a fictional check in the mail or an actor's briefcase, but by directing job contracts my father's way. Did my dad ever become financially wealthy? No, but I never went hungry, and the financial pressure on my parents eased in time.

I can assure you that God is still keeping His word. Today I know Him better than I did at the age of 6. God has replaced my naïveté with a stronger confidence tested by the fires of personal experience. Today He and I have a strong history of answered prayers. Many of you do too.

At a women's retreat in North Dakota one of the women gave a report on the group's yearly project. Besides taking copies of the book *The Desire of Ages*, the story of the life of Christ, to women in the Ukraine, the women of the Dakotas personalized the project by hand-crafting book-markers. Crocheted, knitted, embroidered, petit point — the beautiful works of art came in from all over the area along with a personal letter with each. Knowing the children would feel left out, the women sent along special gifts for them as well.

When packing the contributions for travel, one of the ladies came across a stack of plain celluloid bookmarks one could buy at any Christian supply store. *Oh, well,* she thought. *I guess somebody didn't quite get the idea.*

The project proved to be hugely successful. The women at the first church they visited appreciated the gifts from America. The children did as well. The men waited expectantly for their gift. When none was forthcoming, the translator whispered in the project coordinator's ear, "Don't you have anything for the men? They're feeling left out."

Hastily she passed on the word to one of the other ladies in her group. The women were embarrassed. What should they do? Then she remembered the stack of commercially produced bookmarks. She hurried to the back room and retrieved the bookmarks. The ushers distributed them.

Sheepishly the American women watched as the Ukrainian men studied their little gifts. The bookmarks were all alike, a poem imprinted over a photograph of a beach. The translator read the familiar poem, "Footprints," in Russian.

The eyes of the entire congregation filled with tears when the translator reached the last few lines, "During your times of trial and suffering, when you see only one set of footprints, it was then that I carried you."

The people of the Ukraine understood the anonymous poet's message. They had learned through severe trial that when God says, "Never will I leave you; never will I forsake you," He keeps His word. He can be trusted. His promises are sure.

"That's a lovely story," you might say, "but why do I feel as if my prayers never go beyond the ceiling?"

I wish I could give a quantitative answer to that question. For me, I've learned not to trust my feelings. They're usually faulty. Remember my roller-coaster religion? The highs and the lows? It was based on how I felt from day to day. On good hair days my confidence in God was secure; on PMS days I felt like a spiritual blowout.

I am learning to base my behavior on God's promises instead of my emotions. I am learning to become a woman of devotion instead of a woman of emotion. I am learning that one's experience of new life, of peace, joy, and faith is built, not on a spurt of adrenaline or a surge of endorphins, but upon the solid foundation of biblical truth.

I do not mean to imply that we as women must deny our emotions, one of the lovely qualities of being female. That we should never do. The former presidential aide Charles Colson said, "Christianity is the great leveler." The man who had once prided himself on being tough and calculating did an about-face when he was brought face-to-face with God's love. "I was crying so hard . . . that I couldn't drive the car away. I'd never cried before like that."[1]

Singer, actor, and fellow Christian Robert Goulet says that since he found Jesus, "I cry when somebody drops a Kleenex."[2]

The difference is that my emotions follow spiritual insight, instead of preceding it. My emotional response comes from new insights into God's Word or seeing new evidence of the Holy Spirit working in someone's life.

The combination of studying God's Word and praying for the Holy Spirit produces life-changing results. Guaranteed! The text in Romans about being "transformed by the renewing of your mind" is not just a theory. By following the direction of the Spirit, we put ourselves in the position to receive from the Holy Spirit.

Faith, hope, courage, strength, and power are ours through the avenue of praise.[3] The list of blessings and promises goes on. Whenever I share with others my excitement about the world of praise, abundance, and daughtership, I am afraid I will come on too strong, like a carnival barker hawking magic mirrors or healing potions. The last thing this world needs is another quick fix, another toy box experience. But listen to the words of the One who cannot lie.

Matthew 16:19 says that "whatever you bind on earth will be bound in heaven, and whatever you loose on earth will be loosed in heaven" (NIV).

That's power. Have you ever seen dynamite work? One stick can send a tree stump and its root system high into the sky. A number of sticks can destroy a city block. The keys of the kingdom are dynamite in the hands of a prayer warrior. What unbelievable power for Jesus to put in the hands of mere humans—the same humans who not too long before wanted to pray for fire to come down and consume their enemies.

The apostle Paul described Christ's words as being "the power of God" (Romans 1:16). The Greek word translated power is *dunamis*, from which we get the English word "dynamite."

We'd never give babies dynamite upon which to cut their teeth. But car keys? Babies love to play with car keys. They chew on them, drool on them, shake them to hear them rattle, and clang them against the furniture. But in all the years I've watched babies and keys, never have I seen one crawl to the family Fairlane and start the engine. They haven't a clue as to the power they hold in their drippy little hands. It will take them years before they discover the power in those shiny toys.

Over the years I'd toyed with prayer. I'd given it feeble tries, then wimped out before I learned what it is all about. When my faith was weak, I fell back on the phrase "Well, it must not be the Lord's will." All the while I was like a baby with her daddy's keys. I didn't have a clue how to use them. But when I began asking for the Holy Spirit to live in me, to change my attitudes from scarcity to praise, my prayers fell into line as well.

Prayer combined with praise changes our hearts, not God's. It directs our minds off ourselves and onto God so that we might receive from Him what is rightfully ours as His kids. Perhaps part of our problem is we haven't gotten beyond the infant stage of shaking the keys of the kingdom. We may still not know how to use them properly to start the "engine."

Gumming a car key will never get a baby anything but sore gums. The infant will need to grow physically and intellectually before she is ready to operate an automobile. That is not to say God doesn't answer the prayers of children. On the contrary, I believe God loves building a little one's faith in Him. Why else would He have said, "Let the little children come unto me, . . . for the kingdom of heaven belongs to such as these"? (Matthew 19:14). Their pure, unaffected love is priceless to Him.

Over the years I've been humbled to my knees by the

prayers of innocent children. And chronological age has no bearing on the maturity of a person's spirituality. My daughter Kelli's prayers have moved mountains that I believed impossible to move. Rightly used, the keys can turn the weakest child of God into a prayer warrior, a wimp of a Christian into an overcomer.

[1] William Proctor, *On the Trail of God* (Garden City, N.Y.: Doubleday & Company, Inc., 1977), p. 123.

[2] *Ibid.*, p. 74.

[3] Ellen White, *Christ's Object Lessons* (Mountain View, Calif.: Pacific Press Pub. Assn., 1949), p. 300.

CHAPTER THIRTEEN

The Key Ring

The plastic oval attached to my key ring says "May your car always run as well as your panty hose." Kind of sums up my attitude about life and panty hose. What kind of statement does your key ring make about you? My efficient and practical friend Janice attaches a "club" to her keys so that they can't get lost in the bottom of her purse. My husband keeps his keys on one of those no-nonsense rings that are guaranteed to chip my nails and destroy my cuticles whenever I add or remove a key. Whether made of silver plate, brass, wood, or a leather thong, the ring ties the keys together. To continue the analogy, praise is the ring that holds the keys of God's kingdom together, and faith is the hand that operates those keys.

"I will give you the keys of the kingdom of heaven," Jesus told His disciples after a trying day of grilling by the Pharisees and the Saducees (Matthew 16:19, NIV). But the disciples completely misunderstood what He'd been trying to teach them.

When I read the verses preceding the promise, I get the feeling that Christ's human nature was exhausted from the discourse and needed bolstering. "Who do the people say the Son of Man is?" Jesus asked His disciples.

His friends replied, "Some say John the Baptist; others say Elijah; and still others, Jeremiah or one of the prophets."

The Saviour zeroed in, leaving no room for crawfishing. "But what about you? Who do you say I am?"

"You are the Christ, the Son of the living God" (verses 13-16, NIV). Simon Peter's unwavering declaration of faith must have lifted the Saviour's energy level. How encouraging for Jesus to know that all had not been wasted. Yet the Master could see the crisis nearing, during which even faithful, blustering Peter would deny Him. Peter's inspired confession of faith in Jesus as the Messiah prompted the gift that would turn him and his cohorts into spiritual giants. "I will give you the keys of the kingdom of heaven; whatever you bind on earth will be bound in heaven, and whatever you loose on earth will be loosed in heaven" (verse 19, NIV).

Binding and loosing—let me illustrate how this has worked for a friend of mine. Like most parents, Lynn prays for her daughters regularly. Recently Sue went through some difficult struggles. It was particularly hard for Lynn, Mama Bear, to be 700 miles away—not that she could have done all that much had she lived closer. When Lynn complained to a friend that her prayers were getting nowhere, she asked her how she prayed. Lynn told her. "Lynn, you're using the keys of the kingdom, but not in the way God intended. By telling God how to solve your daughter's problems, you are restricting His creative power."

"Restricting? How?"

"First you hand Sue over to Him, then before He can begin His work, you snatch her back. The text says that what is bound on earth will be bound in heaven, and what is loosed on earth will be loosed in heaven. You've been binding His hands, putting limitations on Him, preventing Him from doing all that He can do for Sue. You need to free His hands so He can get on with His job."

"Free His hands? How do I do that?"

"Do the opposite of what you're doing," she explained. "Loose Sue to Him so He can have complete freedom to do with her as He sees fit."

Visions of tragedy swept through Lynn's mind—crippling accidents, debilitating diseases, horrendous deformities that God might inflict on her in order to "get her attention." You know what I mean. We've all heard it said as we discuss the latest traffic accident in which a brother or sister in Christ was injured. "Sometimes God sends us trouble to get our attention."

What blasphemy! Knowing God as my daddy, I can no longer buy into such a vile theology. James 1:16, 17 clearly tells us what we can expect from our Father. "Don't be deceived, my dear [brothers and sisters]. Every good and perfect gift is from above, coming down from the Father of the heavenly lights, who does not change like shifting shadows" (NIV).

Every good and perfect gift. God does not change like shifting shadows, one day being loving and compassionate, the next vindictive and punishing. Jesus asked, "Which of you, if his son asks for bread, will give him a stone? Or if he asks for a fish, will give him a snake? If you, then, though you are evil, know how to give good gifts to your children, how much more will your Father in heaven give good gifts to those who ask him!" (Matthew 7:9-11, NIV).

Evil comes from the "originator of lies," not Light. Disease, tragedies, and deformities are his specialty, not our heavenly Father's. The God whom we serve is not erratic or inconsistent. He is the great "I Am," the beginning and the end, "the same yesterday, today, and forever."

Old ideas die hard. Lynn struggled with the idea of loosing Sue into God's hands. "I-I-I'm not sure I can do that," she stammered to her prayer warrior friend.

"What is loosed on earth will be loosed in heaven," the woman reminded Lynn. "Remember, God loves Sue much more than you ever can."

God loves Sue more than I do? Impossible, Lynn thought. Yet she knew her friend was right. Of course God loved her daughter more than she ever could. He made her. She was a miracle baby from the night of her conception. Lynn had lost two babies during earlier pregnancies and feared she'd never be able to carry one to full term. Toward the end of her second trimester, her body threatened to miscarry, and she spent three days in the hospital plus another two weeks at home in bed. After Sue was born Lynn and her husband dedicated her to God. *Of course He loves her even more than I do,* Lynn thought, *as impossible as it seems to me.*

That night, on her walk, she looked up at the stars. "OK, Father, I choose to release Sue to You. I loose her from all my artificially imposed restrictions, from all my wishes and desires. I place her freely and completely in Your tender hands. Do with her as You see fit." Lynn took a deep breath, pushed aside the self mumbling inside her, and continued. "I thank You, Father, for answering my prayer to work with my precious daughter. And I praise Your holy name for the wonderful love You have for her, a love that I, as her mother, cannot begin to understand."

Night after night Lynn prayed this prayer. Morning after morning she asked for wisdom to stand back and let God do His thing. Throughout the day, whenever she thought about Sue being so far away and so alone, Lynn asked God to wrap His loving arms about her daughter so she would feel His loving presence in place of her mother's. Then Lynn would follow her request with thanksgiving and praise.

Whenever she was tempted to worry over her situation, Lynn was reminded that she'd given over that "right" to God. Sue was His problem now. Lynn could relax and wait for the results. Through this process Lynn regained the peace she'd lost.

At times, after a particularly disturbing phone call, Lynn would snatch Sue back from God's hands, horrified at the way He seemed to be leading her. Other times she'd try to amend my prayer to include several new stipulations. Then she'd have to loose Sue again to His care. And the process would begin again.

God answered Lynn's prayers, and those of others who were praying for Sue, in exactly the opposite way Lynn imagined possible. And in the process He performed miracles in Sue's spiritual life and in Lynn's, miracles that went beyond a mother's wildest hopes and dreams.

Personally, I am learning not to underestimate the power of prayer. It was Friday afternoon, and Kelli was running late. Everything that could go wrong had, including an out-of-order ATM machine at her usual stop on the way home from work. Needing cash for Sabbath groceries, she drove through heavy Friday afternoon traffic to the next ATM machine. She was waiting in line for her turn at the machine when a woman in her mid-30s approached her.

"Excuse me, but my car broke down. I have enough cash for bus tickets for my two sons, but not for me. I'm embarrassed to ask this, but do you think you could lend me some money so I can get home to Sacramento tonight?"

When Kelli told me this I was thinking, *O God, don't let this woman be snookering her.* Kelli had been working at her job for less than a year. After graduating from college, she'd searched for work for more than a year and a half, hence finances were still tight for her and her husband, Mark.

Without hesitating, Kelli withdrew extra cash from her account and handed it to the woman, along with one of her business cards. "Call me if I can help you in any other way."

The next day Kelli was sitting in church when her business "beeper" sounded. Embarrassed, she shut it off, only to have it beep again as she was walking out of church. Twice more it rang before she could call the number indicated on the machine.

The woman from the ATM was on the phone, asking for another handout. The woman told Kelli that she and her sons had stayed overnight in a cheap motel after a compassionate mechanic volunteered to fix what was wrong with the automobile. While the boss allowed for the man's generosity, he wasn't quite so generous with the towing costs.

Kelli and Mark agreed to take the woman and her sons to the garage to pick up her car after they paid for the towing service. On the way to the garage Kelli apologized for not getting right back to the woman after her first call. "I was in church," Kelli told her. "I couldn't call until I got home to my own phone."

Tears sprang up in the woman's eyes. "I knew it. You must be a Seventh-day Adventist," she said.

Kelli smiled and nodded.

"I could tell. You were so kind to us." She paused and swallowed hard. "I used to be one too."

My first thoughts were *I wonder what mother's prayers were answered that Friday afternoon. I wonder what grandmother who has been faithfully praying for this woman for so many years would give a good old Texas cheer to know about her encounter with Kelli.*

Just as I am sure the Holy Spirit used others to help my daughter Rhonda, He used Kelli to come to the aid of someone else's daughter. A lost and bewildered child of God caught a glimpse of the compassionate Father's face that day. Her prayer warrior may never know how far those seemingly empty prayers went until she reaches the kingdom of heaven.

Probably the most difficult part of this prayer business is maintaining one's faith even when there is no evidence of anything happening. But God's delays are not God's denials.

Year after long year a man, crippled from birth, sat at the Temple gate "Beautiful," begging. When he asked Peter and John for money, Peter said, "Silver or gold I do not have, but what I have I give you. In the name of Jesus Christ of Nazareth, walk" (Acts 3:6, NIV).

As strength returned to the man's legs, he bounded into the Temple leaping and shouting praises. The worshipers stared in amazement at the miracle, giving Peter the opportunity to share the good news of salvation with all the people present. The news of the healing and the subsequent arrest traveled from one corner of Jerusalem to the other.

It is believed that the gate "Beautiful" led from the court of the Gentiles to the court of women on the east wall of the Temple proper.* No doubt Jesus passed through this gate and past the crippled beggar without healing him—time after time. Like many of us desiring immediate answers to our prayers, the beggar might have asked why—why didn't Jesus heal him the first time He saw the deformed legs sprawled out on the Temple steps?

130

Timing—God's timing. The Holy Spirit does all to the glory of God. The crippled man's healing happened in God's time, and thousands learned of the resurrection of His Son as a result.

Praise God, we can be confident that God's timing is perfect. He's never early; He's never late. When we pray with an attitude of praise, we can arise from our knees with a calm assurance that everything is safe in His hands. Any fears we might have had will vanish beyond our curtain of praise.

When the author of Ecclesiastes wrote, "He hath made every thing beautiful in his time," he could have been speaking to the man at the gate. Or he could have been speaking to me when my own father lay dying of cancer. While there's nothing beautiful about cancer, there is everything beautiful about the promised resurrection. As painful as it may be, death isn't the period at the end of life's sentence. Death is but a hyphen separating the good from the best when the faithful will be given new bodies. We will be healed for time and for eternity—in God's time and for His eternity.

---

*Kenneth Barker, ed., *The NIV Study Bible* (Grand Rapids: Zondervan Corporation, 1985), pp. 1648, 1649.

CHAPTER FOURTEEN

Power Tools of Victory

The couple planned a lawn wedding. From twinkling miniature lights scattered throughout the shrubbery to the abundance of flower baskets strewn about, they turned the lawn and poolside into a dreamlike fairyland. A white trellis gazebo separated a small orchestra from the guests. At the far end of the lawn formally dressed waiters scurried to and from the kitchen, carrying silver trays of exquisitely crafted hors d'oeuvres and French canapés to the flower-bedecked, linen-draped tables. A bar complete with imported wines and crystal glassware stood off to one side of the blue-and-white canvas canopy protecting the food.

The ceremony went off as planned, every participant perfectly performing his or her part. As the bride and groom exchanged their vows, the crimson sun touched the blue waters of the nearby bay. The happy couple kissed, and the signal was sent to the professional fireworks expert and his assistants hidden down on the beach. And as planned, when the preacher introduced the radiant couple to the assembled friends and family, the first rocket was lit and soared into the twilight sky.

But in that moment an assistant tossed down his cigarette butt. It landed in one of the cases of fireworks just as a second assistant accidentally tripped, knocking over the same case. The panicky second assistant reached to right his error, but the fireworks expert, recognizing the danger, hauled him back, upsetting the rest of the cases. The resulting show of light and sound far surpassed the couple's wildest imaginations.

The flaming projectiles flew straight toward the wedding party, and pandemonium broke loose. Folding chairs and flower baskets toppled as musicians, wedding attendants, and guests ran for cover. The groom grabbed his bride's hand and ran for the protection of the canopy, joining 20 or so of the guests. But one of the rockets streaked straight through the top of the canvas and severed the center pole. At that, the groom shouted and pushed his new bride toward the exit— and face first into the five-foot-tiered wedding cake. The group could still hear the explosions as the canopy floated down around them, casting them all into total darkness.

The explosives expert and his crew took cover behind a large rock when one after another the cases caught fire, sending rockets in all directions.

Two Navy jets out on maneuvers over the ocean veered off course. Thinking they were under some kind of sniper attack, one of the pilots radioed the control tower at the nearby airport, warning the air controllers to steer all commercial flights clear of the area until the military could check it out.

Before the sky darkened and the last machine gun pop sounded, an entourage of military police and state law enforcement, with sirens blaring, screeched to a stop in front of the father of the bride's wealthy estate.

Fortunately, none of the wedding attendees suffered any serious injuries. The bewildered bridal pair left for their undisclosed honeymoon hideaway amid good-natured taunts of "So how many hours does it take to fly to Baghdad?" and, "Did you pack your bulletproof vests?"

But the honeymooners got the last laugh. With every thank-you note, they included a T-shirt that read "I survived Ann and Bill's wedding."

Great story, but is it true? I believe it's true. The person who told it to me believed it to be true. But to be honest, I don't know. I didn't attend the wedding, and I didn't hear it from a guest at the wedding, either. I heard it through the grapevine, and you know how reliable grapevines can be. They grow everywhere.

We might find a grapevine story entertaining, but we wouldn't want to bet our lives on it. When it comes to life-and-death matters, we want the truth, not embellished fables. And for the truth, we go to the experts. We hire a lawyer for legal matters. We visit a doctor for medical problems. And for spiritual answers, we turn to the Bible.

The victory that comes from living a life of praise is not a "cunningly devised fable." The power that makes victory in Jesus possible for even the weakest of saints is firmly rooted in the Word of God. *Will* is the key. Sin is being out of the will of the Father. You and I are doing either the Father's will or Satan's will. Those are the only two choices.

Matthew 7:21 tells us that "only [he or she] who does the will of the Father [will enter the kingdom of heaven]" (NIV). Victory is ours by doing the will of God. However, tap dancing on golden streets, eating succulent fruit picked from the tree of life, or living forever on Paradise Bay should not be our ultimate goal. Our goal should be the same as that of our Elder Brother, Jesus—living out the will of the Father.

Jesus came to this earth specifically to do His Father's will (John 6:38). And that is "that everyone who looks to the Son and believes in him shall have eternal life" (verse 40, NIV).

That is God's primary will—for His children to be rescued from death. Jesus came to make that happen. "He brought His wishes into strict abeyance to His mission. He glorified His life by making everything in it subordinate to the will of His Father."[1]

Remember the story of the 12-year-old Jesus visiting Jerusalem and becoming separated from His parents? When Joseph and Mary found Him in the school of the rabbis, His mother questioned His behavior. Jesus' reply was the keynote of His life mission—being about His Father's business.

In the most plaintive prayer in the Scriptures (Mark 14:36), Jesus begins by addressing God in the most personal of terms, "Daddy, Father." He follows the address with praise—"everything is possible for you," confessing God's omnipotence. Then the Saviour makes His request: "Take this cup from me." The pain of being separated from His Father by the sins of the world was far more repulsive than the physical pain to be endured. Still, He ends His prayer with "Yet not what I will, but what you will" (verse 36, NIV). His mission was to do the Father's will even unto death.

Jesus said, "Whosoever shall do the will of God, the same is my brother, and my sister, and mother" (Mark 3:35). The problem many of us have is not in wanting to do the will of the Father, but succeeding at it.

When I was 10 and compiled a list of my top 10 sins, the number one on that list was honesty. As I child, I learned to lie to protect myself from parental wrath. And 35 years later I was still protecting myself from censure and disfavor in the same way. Of course, my dishonesty had reached a certain level of sophistication over the years. As an adult, if I couldn't run and hide from confrontation, I wouldn't exactly lie. Instead, I'd weasel out of my predicament with painless half-truths and pleasing innuendos.

As I looked at my own life and the lives of so many struggling brothers and sisters around me, I saw little real victory. Oh, occasionally I'd thrill at the story of the addict who'd overcome drug addiction and the alcoholic for whom the Lord removed the desire for drink. But mostly we all seemed to be just muddling along as best we could, too knowledge-able to reject the truths we knew and too weak to experience real victory. I hated it. I recall praying, "How can I be struggling with the same sins after so many years, Lord? Is there no such thing as victory in You? What do the overcomers referred to in Revelation know that I don't?" But as the Holy Spirit adjusted my attitude, my focus became clearer.

Imagine the work of salvation and the Father's will as a golden city on the far side of a narrow canyon. The chasm separating me from that magical city is deep, the terrain is rugged, and the river at the bottom of the gorge, swift. I've been told that true happiness is available only by living within the city's limits, but I can't find a way to reach the city. I've heard the rumor that there is a bridge upriver called "Praise," but so far I haven't been able to locate it.

Grabbing myself by the scuff of the neck once again, I strap on my bulging backpack and start down the rough mountainside. Loose rock, sheer drop-offs, and exhaustion hamper my progress. By the time I reach the river at the bottom, my bruised muscles scream for rest, but there is no safe place to rest beside the turbulent river. The filth and debris swirling by in the rushing waters nauseate me. I consider turning back, as I've done so many times before. *No,* I think. *This time I'll make it.*

I grit my teeth and dive into the raging river, only to be swept downstream by the powerful current. The weight of my backpack threatens to drag me beneath the raging waters, but somehow I manage to free myself from the current and scramble to the rocks alongside the river, where I fight to catch my breath. Discouraged and defeated, I struggle back up the slippery mountainside. My backpack is now twice as heavy as it had been on the trip down. Once I reach the top, I turn to view the city once more from afar.

That's when I see the discarded guidebook, the cover torn and scuffed with dirt. As I study the enclosed map I discover that the lofty suspension bridge about which I've heard so much is just around the bend. *How have I missed it for so long?*

Buzzards circle in the desert sky above my head as I half stumble, half crawl along the edge of the abyss until I collapse in a heap at the base of a sign. I lift my eyes to read the sign: *No pedestrian traffic allowed!*

I consult my guidebook again and learn that a company called The Cross supplies limousine service for travelers like me. And the Son of the city's Mayor is the chauffeur. I don't have to wait long beside the bridge before I hear people singing. I turn to see a bright-yellow bus overflowing with joyful, happy people coming toward me. When the vehicle pulls alongside of me, the Driver opens the door and asks, "Want a lift to the city?"

"Oh, yes!" I start to climb on board.

"Wait," the Driver says, pointing toward the soggy pack on my back. "There's no room for your pack. Leave it here, and I'll send Someone back for it."

It feels good to drop my pack beside The Cross, but I can't imagine how I'll survive without it. My hopes, my dreams, my heritage—everything that spells "me"—is packed inside it. I hesitate, but then I remember the treacherous chasm and the impassable river. I inhale deeply and climb on board. When the doors swing shut behind me, the people begin singing again. Before we reach the bridge's first support cable, I am caught up in an atmosphere of praise. I barely arrive at the city when the contents of my backpack are delivered to me, sanitized, restored, and purified. And I am home where I belong. I am an overcomer in the name of Jesus Christ.

~

The first and most important element in becoming an overcomer is desiring to do the perfect will of the Father. This desire springs from our inmost being (Ephesians 6:6), what the first-century Greeks called the *psuchē*, from which we get the word "psyche." "God fixes no limits to the advancement of those who desire to be 'filled with the knowledge of his will in all wisdom and spiritual understanding.'"[2]

The second important element happens at our conversion, when we choose to give Him our hearts and lives. Psalm 37:4 tells us, "Delight yourself in the Lord and he will give you the desires of your heart" (NIV). Think a moment. What are the desires of our hearts? A cherry-red Porsche? An electric-blue Ferrari? A mansion atop the wealthy community of "Blooming Hills"?

No, these are desires of our flesh. They change with age, location, and whim. The real desires harbored deep within our inmost beings stay constant or grow stronger with time. I

desire to be saved. I want to live forever in God's perfect kingdom. I made that commitment when I was only 10 years old.

Once we choose to follow the Lord, the promise of
Philippians 1:6 becomes our assurance of God's faithfulness.
"Being confident of this, . . . he who began a good work in
you will carry it on to completion until the day of Christ
Jesus" (NIV).

What a promise for parents whose children stray away
from their youthful convictions. God isn't going to give up on
them. He will strive with them until the day of His coming.

The problem in overcoming is not God's will, but my
will. If I love Him with my whole being (Deuteronomy
30:6), I will want to align my will with His. But how do I do
that? Like the climber trying to ford the raging river, try as
I might, I fail. I usually end up facedown in the slime of my
sins, in a worse condition than I was before I began the
climb. Even after I discovered the bridge of praise, I could
never successfully cross it on my own, no matter how many
choruses of "I'm So Happy in Jesus" I might sing. If overcoming took nothing more than a happy face and a steel will,
the golden city would be populated with fools and despots.

The vehicle that transports my will to the other side can
be nothing but the cross of Christ alone, and the driver,
Jesus, my Saviour. Without the cross, the bridge would be
uncrossable. Throughout the ages millions have attempted to
cross the chasm without acknowledging the cross of Jesus
Christ. Crying, "Lord, Lord," for salvation, but gritting one's
teeth and insisting on doing it "my way," doesn't work.

The last element in my salvation is the one that messes
me up—my backpack of habits, inherited tendencies, and
pet sins. It wears me down, trips me up, and causes me to
stumble. The backpack is too heavy for me to carry to the
other side. I leave it behind so that the Holy Spirit can do
His work. *Choosing to get on board with only my will is the only
real decision I must make.*

"God has given us the power of choice; it is ours to exercise. We cannot change our hearts; we cannot control our

thoughts, our impulses, our affections. We cannot make ourselves pure for His service. But we can choose to serve God,
we can give Him our will; then He will work in us to will and
to do according to His good pleasure. Thus our whole nature will be brought under the control of Christ."[3]

Praise keeps my eyes focused on my goal instead of my
sins. It demonstrates my submission and loyalty to God's
majesty and power. It's only by submission that I can live out
the will of the Father in my life. Yet even my will I can't carry
alone to God. Once I give Jesus permission to carry my will
to the Father, I free the Holy Spirit to clean up the habits and
emotions I've been battling for years. This process isn't a
onetime journey. It must be traveled with every temptation,
at the entry of every one of my death spirals.

On the other side of the gap, the desires of my heart, my
habits, and emotions, as well as my will, must be perfectly
aligned with the will of the Father's (Colossians 4:12). And
I am confident that one day my positive choices will become
automatic. I will have developed the habit of praising. The
spirit of scarcity and fear will be eradicated by the Spirit of
abundance and praise. I will stand "mature and fully assured," without condemnation in the light of the Father's
will—not through my power, but through that of Jesus
Christ. That's the process of salvation. That's real freedom.
That's victory in Jesus. That's overcoming by the blood of
the Lamb.

---

[1] E. G. White, *Life at Its Best*, p. 177.
[2] ———, *The Acts of the Apostles* (Mountain View, Calif.: Pacific Press Pub. Assn.,
1911), p. 478.
[3] Don Matzat, *Truly Transformed*, p. 115.

CHAPTER FIFTEEN

The Perfect Woman
I Want to Be

I want to be a woman, Lord, the perfect blend of
    energy and grace.
I want to be the woman whose lips speak
    wisdom and compassion.
I want to be the woman whose hair is always
    fashion-salon perfect;
Who wears her clothing Barbie Doll-perfect;
Whose nails, complexion, and smile are
    confection-perfect.
Lord, she's the perfect woman I want to be.

~

"Barbie? You gotta be kidding!"

That was my first reaction to a guest on a recent television talk show. The title of the program segment was "Women Who Want to Be Barbie, and the Men Who Love Them." I watched in amazement as the woman proudly displayed an inordinate amount of her body to the television camera. She told how, over a period of time, plastic surgeons had performed 37 surgeries on her body for the sole purpose of molding her into a living replica of the world-famous Mattel toy.

After the woman strutted her stuff across the stage, she admitted that she had two more areas to perfect before reaching her goal—a chin job to sculpt her face from square to oval, and rib surgery to shave two more inches from her waist. Then she declared, "I will be a perfect living Barbie." When the second half of the show—"the men who love them"—was introduced, it has interesting to note that there was not a living Ken doll in sight.

I shook my head in wonder. *Where do they find these kooks, anyway?* Why would any woman in her right mind choose to endure one surgery, let alone 39, to become what she considers the pink of female perfection? At the time I suspected that this woman's first surgery must have been a lobotomy!

My second thought, however, was *Whoa there! Am I so different than she? She's doing nothing more than taking my wishes to extremes.* What woman hasn't, at one time or another, coveted Barbie's slender contours? Those long, perfectly sculpted limbs, the tiny waist, and the to-die-for cheekbones? Even at the mere 7 percent body fat scientists estimate a woman of those proportions would carry, many of us secretly wish we'd inherited the genes and the self-discipline necessary to acquire that severely anorexic figure.

Worse yet, Barbie's 30-something body never shows signs of aging: no smile wrinkles, no sagging jowls, no love handles, and no turkey neck. She remains forever cookie-cutter perfect. Our eyes would be naturally "shadowed" and our bellies ironing-board flat! Imagine!

I confess I'd like that, even if I had to walk on feet designed to wear only five-inch heels.

If God had asked my advice when He formed Eve's soft, gentle curves around the lone rib taken from Adam's side, I would have suggested He mold her out of a Barbie Doll-shaped, age-repellent plastic instead of biodegradable protein. Then His perfect woman would have been beautiful for all eternity.

If I were creating a new and perfect world, I'd make it one giant toy box of perfect Kens and blemish-free Barbies. Without human passions and pride, there'd be no poverty, no killing fields, no tiny bodies with bellies distended by malnutrition. Bosnia, Rwanda, or Rhode Island—we'd all reside in Barbie townhouses and dine on Chippendalereplica tables laden with Barbie linen, Barbie china, and Barbie silverware. We'd vacation at Barbie Malibu beach houses, go camping in Barbie motor homes, and drive Barbie sports cars to and from our perfect, upscale Barbie-type jobs. Just imagine!

As creator, I would have installed within our perky synthetic heads a microchip that would, when triggered, repeat, "I love you, darling. I love you." The microchip could be programmed to contain no negative words. No child would ever hear a parent say "I wish you'd never been born." No mate would suffer the heart-slashing curse of "I don't love you anymore." No parent would longingly wait for the phone call that never comes.

No cries of rape, murder, or war would ever be heard. Hate, envy, and greed wouldn't exist. Our plastic-cast smiles would never fade. Tears would never flow from our unseeing eyes. And our hearts would never break. We'd be perfect women and men living perfect lives. Yes, that's how I would have populated my perfect world.

> I want to be a wife, Lord, the comfort of
>   her husband,
> Playful, eager, forever young . . .
> I want to be the wife who never complains
>   or nags,
> Who lifts burdens from his shoulders instead
>   of adding to them.
> I want to be the wife, Lord, who never gets her
>   feelings hurt,
> Who never holds a grudge,
> Who is always ready to listen with her heart.
> Lord, she's the perfect wife I want to be.

~

During my teenage years my girlfriends and I resolved that we would be perfect wives when we married our perfect husbands. We dwelt in the fairy-tale age of bobby pins,

Dippity-Do, naïveté, and vanishing creams. My friend Ruthie vowed she'd never, ever let her husband see her hair in "rollers." Anna assured us that she would awaken at least a half hour before her husband each morning so that he'd never find her without her makeup skillfully applied.

Along with affirming Ruthie's and Anna's pledges, I voiced emphatic opinions about wives who "let themselves go," wives who used mixes instead of cooking from scratch, and wives who went to bed angry. How immature such women were! *I* knew that my future husband and I would never argue. We would always be patient, reasonable, and forgiving. Like Mattel's Barbie and Ken, we'd have a perfect marriage.

Today I recall my childish notions and smile. At that time I didn't have a clue what living and loving was all about. My swarthy knight has seen me in curlers, rollers, and a whole lot worse. In spite of the worst, our love has grown through hard work and tears, and not because of my famous made-from-scratch macaroni and cheese casseroles. When it comes to "letting go," both of us have bitten our own tongues often enough to require transplants. While we try never to go to bed angry, there have been a few late-night sessions when our bleary, bloodshot eyes have seen the first rays of dawn. Our marriage of 30-plus years has been good, but alas, not perfect.

I'm not the wife I want to be. At times I'm a total discomfort to Richard. All the things I vowed I wouldn't do, I've done. I don't like the crone who occasionally replaces the coquette my husband married, the woman who complains, nags, sags, and holds grudges. This is not the wife I dreamed of becoming. This is not the perfect wife I want to be.

Sometimes in my lingering childishness I ask, "Lord, why didn't You make me so that I could not fail, so I'd never disappoint my husband, so I'd always be perfect—not just in outward appearance, but perfect within?" Like my birthday text of Proverbs 31, I want to possess a delicate blend of energy and grace that would "do him good and not evil all the days of my life" (see verse 12). I wish I always spoke with wisdom and compassion.

Then I recall the story of Eden and the perfect woman carved by God's own hand. And I recall the love that allowed her to make choices. I too make choices.

> I want to be a mother, Lord, the pride of
>   her children . . .
> Joyful, understanding, and overflowing with
>   self-control.
> I want to be the mother who never yells, scolds,
>   or heaps on the guilt.
> I want to be the mother whose kitchen is always
>   stocked with homemade cookies and home-
>   spun wisdom.
> Lord, she's the perfect mother I want to be.

Like most little girls, I played dress-up in my mother's clothing. I'd place her black-felt, go-to-meeting hat on my straight brown hair and slip the blush veil down over my freckled nose. Then I'd step into her black, size 8 church shoes, the ones with the sensible Cuban heels. (My mother always wore sensible shoes.) Then I'd prance in front of her bedroom mirror and admire the effect from every angle. Unfortunately, the hat drooped over one eye, and the flowered silk dress dragged on the floor behind me. *Someday,* I promised myself, *I'll grow up and fit my mama's clothes—perfectly.*

As I grew into my teens, I discovered that my mother wasn't so perfect after all. I looked at my friends' mothers and passed harsh judgment on my own. I developed a new image of the woman I believed to be the perfect mother, the mother I'd become one day.

Patient, tender, gentle, loving, always there for my children, always meeting their needs before meeting my own—that would be me. I would "watch over the affairs of my household." My children would "rise up and call me blessed" (see verses 27, 28). And like the television moms of the fifties, there'd always be a hot apple pie cooling in the pantry and a full jar of chocolate-chip cookies in the cupboard. And I'd be wearing my daisy-print housedress, my freshly starched apron, and my five-inch heels.

Reality hit in the form of two "perfect" daughters. While I struggled to polish my image of the perfect mom, they zeroed in on the chinks in my plastic-coated armor—to mix a few metaphors. My stress increased when I saw those chinks reflecting back at me through my daughters' behavior. Too often I saw my mother's face smiling at me in the mirror, especially the morning Rhonda cried, "Mother, stop trying to be God!"

Her accusation rang in my ears as I skittered away to my bedroom to nurse my injured heart. And there, face-to-face with myself and my God, I realized she was right. I was trying to play God in everyone's lives. I was trying to convince her and myself that I was all-knowing, all-seeing, without flaw, perfection incarnate. *But isn't that what You want of me, Lord? To do what I can to solve their problems? To be an example for them?*

There in the mirror I saw the real me. If I ever wanted to reach my daughter in honesty, I would have to admit that the perfect wonder woman, wife, and mother I'd imagined myself to be was a fantasy left over from childhood. I'd been playing house, frantically trying to fool myself, the world, and my family—none of which were deceived.

> I want to be a sister, Lord, always there for Connie
>   and Val, as well as for my sisters in Christ . . .
> Dependable, cheerful, hospitable.
> I want to be the sister who is never jealous, never
>   petty, and never small-minded.
> I want to be the sister who never tears others
>   down, but instead builds up.
> Lord, she's the perfect sister I want to be.
>
> I want to be a friend, Lord, a neighbor to the
>   world . . .
> Concerned, caring, and never too busy to help.

I want to be the friend who never gossips and
    never competes.
I want to be the friend who sees the world
    through Jesus' eyes, then cares enough to
    change things.
Lord, she's the perfect friend I want to be.

I want to be a professional woman, Lord, a role
    model for the young,
    but never at the expense of her family . . .
Smart, successful, and competent.
I want to be the professional who achieves her goals
    without forfeiting her ethics or her charm.
I want to be the professional who rises to the top,
    but never loses sight of who she is and how she
    got there.
Lord, she's the perfect professional woman I want
    to be.

～

As a sister, a friend, and as a professional, I skillfully
drape the perfect multicolored scarf about my neck to fit
each occasion. A phone call, a letter, a speaking engagement,
and I don the correct scarf to enhance the correct outfit that
makes me look like the woman I want to be. Some scarves I
wear are frayed and worn, while the patterns of others are
woven with threads of gold and silver. Flashy, subdued,
playful, outrageous—they're all me. And no matter how
kind, how considerate, how witty and clever I may have
been that day, when I remove my scarf and see my reflection
in the mirror, I see a woman with a smudge on her chin and
a "beam" in her eye, revealing the bratty child hiding within,
the daughter who still can't quite get it right.

I want to be Your daughter, Lord, an honor to
    Your name.
Simple, eager, and tender.

I want to be the daughter who never questions
    Your wisdom and never doubts Your love.
I want to be the daughter who rests securely in
    Your arms and wholly trusts Your leading.
Lord, she's the perfect daughter I want to be.

～

As a child, I desperately wanted to be perfect. Yet no matter how hard I tried, I ripped the hems out of my dresses, muddied my shoes, ratted my hair, and dirtied my face. Other children seemed to instinctively know how to make the right move, say the proper words, and take the wisest actions. Was I the only kid who couldn't quite get the rules of the game right? By the time my skills improved, someone changed the rules and I became a teenager. Then just as I could maneuver the obstacle course of the teens, I swung into my 20s, leaping into adulthood with the satellite games of wifedom and motherhood. And were the rules of those games ever complicated! All the while the desire of my heart was to be God's perfect daughter, a blend of Barbie on the outside and the virtuous wife of Proverbs 31 on the inside.

If a toy company designed a doll that epitomized real women, one with split ends, graying hair, and age spots, it wouldn't sell. Who'd buy a chubby, churlish reality doll for their child? a doll riddled with dysfunctions, compulsions, and obsessions? If the toymakers considered a line of reality dolls fashioned after women of the nineties they would need to include a Single Parent Barbie, one who slings hash at Joe's Cafe while attending night classes to complete her GED. Her accessories could include an Absent Father Ken and three hungry babies. Another reality doll would be a Recovering Barbie with an abusive Alcoholic Ken and a Runaway Skipper. And, of course, for the overachievers, they'd design a Super Barbie that could be wound up into a frenzy. She would operate on instantly rechargeable batteries, but would crash into a thousand pieces on the seventh major crisis of each day.

Such projects would be doomed for failure because Mattel isn't selling plastic dolls as much as they are selling celluloid dreams—the dream of perfection. But such a dream is impossible without God.

CHAPTER SIXTEEN

God's Barbie Dolls

One day as I was walking along the beach in Santa Cruz I read a disturbing message graffittied on a seawall. *I've forgotten what it's like to feel decent; therefore, nothing I do really matters.*

From the top of the wall to the bottom, the writer repeated this sentence again and again, until the words disappeared into the sand. Why? What had precipitated this person's feelings of hopelessness? What crimes had this individual committed that made them hate themself so? How far had they fallen from the image of the person they considered decent? Did they or had they ever known a God who loves and forgives? What self-disgust drove them to bare their heart to the world?

A friend of mine, a scholar in biblical languages, shared with me a new perspective to an old favorite, John 3:16. "For God so loved . . . that whosoever believeth . . . would not perish . . ." The word "perish" in Greek is *apollumi,* which implies the completion of the process of destruction, or, as my friend put it, "whosoever believeth . . . would not self-destruct." The idea that all sin eventually leads to self-destruction ping-ponged off the walls of my brain for many days.

I thought about the frantic 20-mile drives I'd made as a girls' dean to the closest hospital to save the lives of girls who'd overdosed on medication. Almost without exception, they hated themselves and the mistakes they'd made. They'd rather end it all than live with the persons they'd become. I remembered my own moments of despair, and those of close friends teetering on the verge of self-destruction.

"Be ye therefore perfect," Jesus said, "as your Father which is in heaven is perfect" (Matthew 5:48). Perfection is a subject guaranteed to stir the hearts of every born-again and not-so-born-again Christian. We crave it. We discuss it. We study it. We strive for it. We think we understand it. And when we don't, we play games, pretending we have it.

But have you noticed that when people get hung up on the subject of perfection they seldom exhibit the fruit of the Spirit—the character of Christ? Their love and their patience with others' opinions and mistakes disappear in a barrage of rhetoric.

However, it isn't all bad, this desire our perfect Father placed within us. The desire for perfection drives people like Handel to compose the *Messiah*, Ansel Adams to shoot the perfect photograph, Michelangelo to sculpt a perfect *David*, and the apostle John to write about the life of Jesus Christ. And while the end result may be trivial to you and me, to the woman who set her heart on becoming the perfect living Barbie, her desire for perfection was no less intense. She willingly faced possible death with every nip and tuck of the surgeon's knife. She risked life itself to maintain her anorexic figure. Unfortunately, the pleasure of reaching her goal will be short-lived, for time and gravity will rearrange her playing field. And her obsession with perfection will once again wreak havoc with her peace and joy.

So many women have shared with me their frustrations with trying desperately to be perfect and failing so badly. Andrea poses as a "beige lady." You know the ones—those graceful creatures who match perfectly from the tips of their Gucci shoes to their platinum-blond French twists. Inside Andrea hides a dirty little waif who can never do anything right. My friend Sarah admits to covering up her insecurities with a frenzy of religious activity until she finds herself worn out and discouraged. "I feel as though I'm trapped in a giant game of chess and I'm the only pawn on the board. I can't go on, but I can't escape, either."

Sound familiar?

Camille has enough honesty to admit that she points her finger at others' foibles, hoping no one will notice the imperfections in her own holy facade. Irene frantically seeks spiritual highs through the latest exposés of fellow Christians. Susan buys into the newest sensational spin on an obscure point of doctrine as proof of her devotion to the Word of God, trying to fill the hole in her soul. Amy preaches the latest prediction of the day, time, or year of Christ's return to all who will listen. She can't understand why her number of listeners are dwindling.

Kim periodically "kicks over the traces," as my mother used to say, and walks away from the family of God, only to, a few weeks later, resume her game. "I know I'm lost," she says. Her voice and face are devoid of emotion. "I've been in the church for 27 years. During that time I've filled almost every church office there is. I've led out in the children's department every week for the past 10 years." The tissue in her fists is in damp shreds. "To tell the truth, I don't know why I do it. Because in the end, I know I'm not saved and I never will be."

The pain in her voice echoes Susan's, Camille's, and Amy's. "Be ye perfect," Jesus said in Matthew 5:48. The despair these women feel of ever reaching perfection burns across the spectrum of age. Believing themselves neither saved nor lost, neither enjoying the sins of the world for a season nor living the abundant life Jesus promised, they beg for time-out in the frenzied game of church, a time-out long enough to get it all together. They believe that their only hope is that one day Jesus will change them in an instant, yet they doubt such a miracle can ever occur.

> Someday I'll meet her, Lord, the wife and mother,
> the sister and friend—the woman I want to be.
> She'll be wearing my freckles.
> She'll be sporting my grin.

And she'll be lifting one eyebrow in whimsical
   disbelief.
Someday I'll turn around and there she'll be—
The perfect woman I want to be.

~

Unfortunately, it's all wrong. Our loving Father didn't
leave us to stumble along in our sins, with Paradise our only
hope. Like little children slipping into a cardigan sweater, we
have it inside out. We're trying to wear our Christian label on
the outside instead of on the inside, where it belongs.

During the late seventies my daughters got caught up in
the designer jeans craze. Kelli, especially, found the designer
label very important, more important than fit or comfort.
When our family went through a financial crisis and designer
jeans were a thing of the past, she had to settle for jeans with
labels that were less prestigious among her friends.

One day I walked into her room and found her sewing.
I was stunned. It's not that Kelli couldn't sew (she could),
but to do so willingly? She was sewing a designer label from
her worn-out jeans onto her less-expensive new ones. She
and her friends hadn't yet learned that quality is determined
by construction, fabric, and fit rather than by brand name.

The same is true of people. Character isn't determined
by the brand worn on the outside. Thinking that a Christian
is a Christian because he or she is kind, loving, and considerate toward others implies that anyone who is a "giving"
person must therefore be a Christian.

"In 1948, in the midst of an Arab-Israeli conflict, one high-
ranking U.S. government official allegedly said, 'If these Arabs
and Jews would sit down around a bargaining table and act
like good Christians we wouldn't have all this difficulty!'"[1]

"What a misconception—that a Christian is a kind, loving and considerate person because he is a Christian. First,
he must become a Christian and receive God's life-changing
love and kindness. Only then—as a result of being transformed by God—can he pass on the same love and kindness

to others. Christians love because they have been receivers of God's love for them."[2]

What matters to God is what's inside our hearts, not our outward appearance and actions. The other way around, while it matches the world's standards, isn't God's way. When we believe it is, we are spiritually delusional. We have confused fact with fantasy; the real with the pretend; God's perfect character with Hollywood's concept of perfection.

God hasn't given me a long list of things to do and not to do. While the Bible gives instruction on conduct, God never intended for me to fulfill His laws by way of willpower and resolution. My Father gave me one task—to abide in Christ Jesus! "I'd been so busy shaking off the old leaves by the use of my willpower, but without success, when what I wanted was to bear fruit."[3]

Jesus Christ warned His disciples about the delusions of living inside out. He said that we needed to lose our lives to find them; to give if we wished to receive; to be last if we wanted to be first. He showed us that the kingdom of God is spiritual, not physical. He compared the Pharisees' righteousness to "whited sepulchres," lovely on the outside but inside containing nothing but dead bones. To the world these men appeared holy, but the Son of God could see that their righteousness was like filthy rags (Isaiah 64:6).

As women we can appreciate more than our brothers just how disgusting a human's self-righteousness must be to God. The filthy rags referred to by Isaiah are actually the cloths a woman used during her menstrual period, a time when she was considered unclean by Jewish society and had to separate herself from the clan. We've all been inconvenienced and embarrassed by "life's little inconveniences." I can't think of anything that could reduce me to tears quicker. I remember my mother telling me about the days before Kimberly-Clark, how the soiled cloths would have to be soaked, then washed and hung out to dry after each period—a repulsive task to be sure.

How much worse it was for the women of Christ's day.

Yet, regardless of when in the course of history a woman lived, the analogy reveals clearly God's view of our self-righteous acts—male or female.

In our upside-down world, we too often reclassify human mistakes as sins and sanitize our sins by calling them mistakes. We measure perfection by the outward appearance, while God looks on the heart (Isaiah 16:7).

Let me give you an example. I was running late for a class. I grabbed my purse and my books and headed toward the front door when the telephone rang. It was a long-distance call from a friend who'd recently lost a son in a car accident. I couldn't rush her. She reached out to me, and I had to be there for her. I listened and watched the hands of the clock inch closer to 7:00, the time my class was scheduled to start.

After several minutes, when I was sure that she was feeling better, I explained my problem to her, promising to call her back the moment I returned home. Being a good friend, she understood. I hung up the receiver and rushed out the door. In record time I reached the school parking lot. I drove up and down the rows searching for an empty space until I found one in the "back forty."

Switching out of my heels into my running shoes, I dashed across the parking lot and up the steps to the causeway that ran the length of the campus. I joined the mob of students and faculty members rushing through the long open-air mall that linked the fourplex classroom "learning pods" with one another.

I glanced at my watch as I weaved in and out of the surging mass of humanity. As I passed a ladies' restroom, I thought, *I'll be teaching or helping students straight through the three-hour classtime. Late or not, I'd better duck in here while I have the chance.*

Within a short time I was racing down the corridor again. A number of stragglers watched as I hurried past. Breathless, I rushed into the classroom, apologizing for my tardiness. "I'll write your evening assignment on the board and let you get started," I told them. "It will give me time to catch my breath and take record."

I whirled about and scribbled the evening's topic on the board. When I turned back to face the class, the men in the class had one hand up to their foreheads as if shading their eyes, while the women were gesturing wildly and pointing toward my skirt. Bewildered, I shrugged and pulled out the teacher's chair. When I went to smooth the back of my skirt to sit down, there was no skirt. And there was no slip, just pantyhose.

During my short pit stop, my skirt had gotten tucked into the waistband of my pantyhose. I'd run the length of the campus in that condition. It was a human mistake—fortunately not one of life-threatening proportions (except to my dignity).

Both sin and human error are involved in this story. In my haste I discovered again that I was human. I made a dumb mistake, not checking to be certain my skirt was straight before leaving the restroom. However, if I'd been abrupt with my friend on the telephone, if I'd been uncaring and brushed her aside, that would not only have been a mistake; it would have been a sin.

God is love. My commission as a child of God is to "be" love in the place of the Father. "Love one another, as I have loved you," Jesus tells us. Love is what God wants us to demonstrate for Him—love for God and love for other people. When I don't love, I sin.

The Pharisees of Jesus' day strictly adhered to the ceremonial laws. They tithed every herb produced in their gardens. They measured to the inch the distances they could walk on the Sabbath day, but they had no concept of loving others. They'd rescue an animal from a pit on the Sabbath day, but heal a paraplegic? Never!

Human mistakes can be costly. In the instance of my friend's son, a youthful error cost him his life. However, a sin is a sin is a sin, and it can cost us not only our temporal life but eternity as well. Too often we berate ourselves for our stupid mistakes while overlooking our sins, euphemistically

calling them foibles or little white lies. But understand this—
God's children must call sin by its right name.

The adulterous woman thrown at His feet, the woman at
the well, Nicodemus—the Master had a way of getting past the
surface problem and zeroing in on the person's genuine need.

Isaiah 59:2 says, "Your iniquities have separated you
from your God" (NIV). Not our mistakes, but our iniquities.
My pantyhose experience was not a sin against God. It did
not separate me from my Father. I even imagined that He
got as big a laugh over it as my family did later that evening.

This, though, is sin: "Your hands are stained with blood,
your fingers with guilt. Your lips have spoken lies, and your
tongue mutters wicked things" (verse 3, NIV).

The Holy Spirit is a Spirit of discernment. He will "lead
us into all truth" about ourselves and the world around us.
He will reveal to us the motives behind our actions. This
way we will be able to discern the difference between sin
and error. His task is to turn our thinking inside out to
match the Father's.

Sometimes we grow impatient. We want patience, and
we want it now! We want perfection now! But I've noticed
over the years that God seldom grants us our talents fully
developed. The same is true with character development. By
praying "I praise You, Lord. Show me Your will today," we
facilitate the process of perfecting our character. Perfection,
the Greek word *teleios*, means "finished, complete, mature."

The process of maturing spiritually or the perfection of
one's character deals directly with our sins. The process of
maturing physically, emotionally, and intellectually deals
with the process of learning from our mistakes or human errors. We do not need to worry and fret over the matter. We
do not need to lose our peace and our joy. We can trust our
Father to carry out His promise. "The Lord will perfect that
which concerneth me: thy mercy, O Lord, endureth for
ever" (Psalm 138:8). He will send the Holy Spirit to teach us
when to forgive ourselves for our mistakes and when to trust
God to forgive us of our sins.

Someday I'll meet her, Lord, the wife and mother,
    the sister and friend—the woman I want to be.
She'll be wearing my freckles.
She'll be sporting my grin.
And she'll be lifting one eyebrow in whimsical
    disbelief.
Someday I'll turn around and there she'll be—
The perfect woman I want to be.

But until then, Lord, make me willing each day,
To be the woman *You* want me to be.
Anoint my eyes with compassion,
My ears with tolerance,
And my heart with joy.
Let me grow in Your grace.
Let my every word and my every deed be as
    pure and clear and transparent as sunlight.
May I live each moment to glorify Your
    holy name.
Lord, that's the kind of woman You can create
    in me.

---

[1] D. Matzat, *Truly Transformed* p. 115.
[2] *Ibid.*
[3] *Ibid.*, p. 20.

CHAPTER SEVENTEEN

Getting Real With God

*M*elts in your mouth, not in your hand." During World War II the Mars candy company manufactured a candy that would be convenient for the troops to carry. They encased chocolate droplets in sugar shells. And so M&Ms were born.

Every M&M connoisseur knows there are rules of proper etiquette for eating M&M candies. First, true afficionados never settle for generic M&Ms. For that matter, they are seldom willing to consider the M&M alternate product, candy-coated peanuts or almonds.

When true M&M fanciers open a new bag of candies, they will line up the M&Ms in pairs by color. The candies must be devoured in the proper order, by color: light brown, dark brown, yellow, orange, green, then red. Yet even the most avid M&M lover will tell you that there's no difference in flavor between the red and the yellow or the brown candies.

I have discovered that in the home of every M&M gourmet lives at least one M&M cretin. This person lies in wait for the connoisseur to complete the ritual, then pounces, destroying the perfect little pattern the connoisseur created. Rhonda and I are the M&M connoisseurs in our family. I'll let you guess the identities of the cretins.

Sugar-coated shells are great for chocolate candy, but highly destructive for the sons and daughters of God—no matter how sweet the covering might be. Coatings for Christians come in rich and poor, educated and unschooled, male and female (and the list goes on). These shells protect me from the messy world outside my immediate sphere. They allow me to spout noble-sounding clichés about love for others without the risk of getting my hands dirty. I can hide behind my politically correct caricature of what God intended for me spiritually.

God is anointing His people—those who choose to live in the will of God—to go and tell of His loving-kindness. Before we can carry out our privilege, we must first allow Him to melt our shells "with lovingkindness" (Jeremiah 31:3). We must become vulnerable to others. There is no other way to live God's love. There is no other way to "preach" the gospel. We will either become vulnerable or fossilize.

Knowing that we are secure in God's hands allows us to melt our protective coatings. Teenagers of the nineties say, "Get real!" The Bible indicates that we must learn to be rigorously honest with God, each other, and with ourselves. Jesus implied, perhaps with some sarcasm toward His listeners, that even God cannot heal us unless we know we need a physician (Matthew 9:12,13).

Ironically, by allowing God to melt our generic shells, we become unique, one of a kind, Designer creations. Getting real is the only way we can reach out and touch one another's hearts. One of my favorite writers calls it becoming "as transparent as the sunlight."[1]

For a child who had so much difficulty admitting the truth about herself, I have come to regard this analogy as precious. I keep the phrase before my eyes constantly—above my computer, in my Bible, on my refrigerator, all the places I frequent.

Learning to be honest, inside and out, is scary. Sometimes the truth is unpleasant. Sometimes it hurts. It is possible only when I am guided by the Holy Spirit. But the rewards are incredible.

I would describe my husband and me as a civilized couple. We don't argue in public. We don't throw things at each other or kick, scream, or pinch when angry. We respect each other enough never to belittle each other to others, or to belittle our relationship. But before we discovered the beauty of being "transparent as sunlight," we had a major problem—admitting the truth, telling each other how we really felt.

Maybe this never happens to you, but for us, the problem usually started when partner 1 said, "You want to eat out tonight?"

Rather than offend, partner 2 would not admit that he/she was exhausted and preferred to kick back in an easy chair with a good book. Instead, he/she answered, "Sure. What do you have in mind?"

Here's where partner 1 joined in the deceit. "No place special. What are you hungry for?" Of course, partner 1 had something in mind. He/she wouldn't have brought up the subject if he/she didn't.

"I don't know. You decide." This dialogue could continue for several minutes. And if partner 2 was experiencing extra stress in his/her life, the conversation could end in an argument—an argument between two people who only wanted to be thoughtful of each other.

Being transparent as sunlight can stop this deception, for now we are not afraid to speak the truth in love. I can dare to be vulnerable with Richard, and he can be completely vulnerable with me. In the process, the honesty has removed many of the barriers that kept our marriage from growing.

Honesty in love comes with qualifications. It is never used to win an argument or to one-up the other person. It can work only through love and humility.

"The fear of facing real fears is almost universal. All my life my own fears of facing anger, guilt, loneliness, hurt or other feelings accompanying failure and sin made the kind of spiritual growth that leads to authentic character change impossible for me. I had a real fear of having people know my faults."[2]

I talked about "transparent" living in a witness seminar I conducted. After the class a woman introduced herself as a fellow writer. Using my admonition for honesty, she told me that she didn't approve of one of the books I'd written. I could tell by her hesitancy that she wasn't comfortable confronting me. That's all right. I wasn't comfortable having her do so. However, the results of her honesty were rewarding to both of us. I was given the opportunity to explain my reasons for writing the book as I did, and she could better understand and appreciate my reasons. We parted as sisters and fellow sufferers in the publishing world.

During one of Mother Teresa's visits to the United States to raise money for her mission in Calcutta, she recited the following prayer during an interview on Robert Schuller's television program, *Hour of Power.*

"Lord, make my life a window for Your light to shine through, and a mirror to reflect Your love to all I meet." That sounds like transparency to me, living a life with every thought, deed, and motive transparent as sunlight.

Our churches face an "honesty crisis." We try so hard to appear like the ideal "happy face" Christian that we fail miserably in being honest and compassionate with one another. As one writer put it, "Christianity [should be] one beggar telling another beggar where he found bread."[3]

∼

The only way we can touch another life is to allow our inner selves to be touched. There's no room for ego. When God's Word speaks of humility, it isn't a cringing, wimpish trait of character. Humility recognizes our humanity and God's divinity, and we praise God for that difference. Forgiveness begets humility, and humility begets praise. We see ourselves as we really are and are overwhelmed with gratitude for His saving power.

"God is able to make all grace [including the melting of our shells] abound in you, so that in all things at all times, having all that you need, you will abound in every good work" (2 Corinthians 9:8, NIV).

A minister checking out at the local grocery store was

startled to discover that his bill came to several dollars more than he'd expected. Before leaving the checkout station, he glanced over the bill and noticed he'd been charged for items he hadn't purchased. When he asked about the discrepancy, the clerk agreed to ring up the man's purchases a second time. This infuriated the customer waiting in line behind him, and she let him know it in a voice worthy of the Broadway stage. Other people in the line began to grumble also.

While the clerk found and corrected the error, the embarrassed minister apologized to the other customers for the inconvenience. However, the apology or the fact that a mistake had been made didn't appease one woman. Her strident comments followed the poor man out of the store.

As he was loading his grocery bags into the trunk of his car, one of the customers went out of his way to say, "Sir, you wear your religion well."

While the customer did not know the man was a pastor, he did know that the man was a Christian. That's what was important. By being humble and not snarling back at the woman, the pastor had taken the risk of vulnerability. He'd been ridiculed for His Master. And in the process he'd given God his highest praise by glorifying the Father's name before those who watched it all happen.

The man's vulnerability didn't come naturally. It was as much a miracle as when Jesus healed the paraplegic or raised Lazarus from the grave. It was the miracle of a God-changing life.

While we can never boast about victory as if it were our doing—it's always by His grace—we have guaranteed success! Every time.

"'No eye has seen; no ear has heard, no mind has conceived what God has prepared for those who love him'—but God has revealed it to us by his Spirit" (1 Corinthians 2:9, NIV).

Talk about a spiritual high! This one's a "keeper." It's mine now and for all eternity. I can be confident in my salvation. I need never climb back inside my rigid little toy box again. I am free! Free to dare the impossible—"to go where no one has gone before."

"Whoa! Wait a minute here. Why all this excitement and all this praise? If only it were so easy," I hear you say. It's true. While new growth brings the awareness of new joy, it also uncovers layers of difficulties and problems about ourselves that we never before faced.

The biblical truth of the matter is that when we surrender our lives to God, when we shed our sugar coatings, when we dare to take God to the limits, our spiritual muscles won't atrophy. We *will* have problems (Romans 7:7-25). We will need continually to cross the bridge of praise, lining up our will with the Father's. We will continue to need His forgiveness and His grace until the day comes when the spiritual kingdom of God merges with the physical kingdom of God, and we see Him face-to-face.

In the meantime, our loving Father will keep His word. He will continue to pull it all together until we are complete—the mental, physical, emotional, and spiritual children He envisioned when He knelt in Eden's soil. One day we will be mature in Christ. On that day He will bestow on us "a crown of glory that fadeth not away" (1 Peter 5:4). We will join those who have "washed their robes, and made them white in the blood of the Lamb" (Revelation 7:14).

All our questions will be answered. All the arguments over perfection and over the nature of Christ's character will be settled. All will know for certain that our Father is God and that He can be trusted. And we will be so filled with love for Him that we will praise His name throughout all eternity.

As one of my favorite authors put it, "the day is coming when the battle will have been fought, the victory won. The *will of God is to be done on earth as it is done in heaven.* All will be a happy, united family, *clothed with the garments of praise and thanksgiving—the robe of Christ's righteousness.* All nature . . . will offer to God a tribute of praise and adoration."[4]

I am so thankful that God has granted us, His children, the right to worship Him through our praise, to "try on" our robes of Christ's righteousness for size, here and now. I like knowing that I can be confident of the "fit." I am overwhelmed with love when I remember where I was and where He has led me.

As much as I appreciate surprises, I would hate to reach the gates of the heavenly kingdom and discover I didn't qualify to enter because of some obscure, unknown rule that the Father forgot to reveal to me. I would loathe missing out on eternity because of a new rule in some religious card game.

We can have confidence in our salvation today. We can live in the kingdom of God now. Not because of our goodness, but because of the Father's goodness. Not through our sacrifices, but through the blood of Jesus Christ. Not through our power, but through the power of the Holy Spirit working out the will of God in our lives.

> "Blessed assurance, Jesus is mine!
> O, what a foretaste of glory divine!
> Heir of salvation, purchase of God,
> Born of His Spirit, washed in His blood.
>
> "This is my story, this is my song,
> Praising my Savior all the day long;
> This is my story, this is my song,
> Praising my Savior all the day long."[5]

---

[1] Ellen White, *Thoughts From the Mount of Blessing* (Mountain View, Calif.: Pacific Press Pub. Assn., 1964), p. 68.

[2] J. K. Miller, *Sin*, p. 142.

[3] D. T. Niles, in *Simpson's Contemporary Quotations*. (Boston: Houghton Mifflin & Company, 1988), p. 193.

[4] E. G. White, *Life at Its Best*, pp. 302, 303. (Italics supplied.)

[5] Fanny Crosby, "Blessed Assurance."

She's the Perfect Woman
I Want to Be

I want to be a woman, Lord, the perfect blend of
    energy and grace.
I want to be the woman whose lips speak wisdom
    and compassion.
I want to be the woman whose hair is always
    fashion-salon perfect;
Who wears her clothing Barbie Doll-perfect;
Whose nails, complexion, and smile are
    confection-perfect.
Lord, she's the perfect woman I want to be.

I want to be a wife, Lord, the comfort of
    her husband,
Playful, eager, forever young . . .
I want to be the wife who never complains
    or nags,
Who lifts burdens from his shoulders instead
    of adding to them.
I want to be the wife, Lord, who never gets her
    feelings hurt,
Who never holds a grudge,
Who is always ready to listen with her heart.
Lord, she's the perfect wife I want to be.

I want to be a mother, Lord, the pride of
    her children . . .
Joyful, understanding, and overflowing with
    self-control.
I want to be the mother who never yells, scolds,
    or heaps on the guilt.
I want to be the mother whose kitchen is always
    stocked with homemade cookies and home-
    spun wisdom.
Lord, she's the perfect mother I want to be.

I want to be a sister, Lord, always there for Connie
and Val, as well as for my sisters in Christ . . .
Dependable, cheerful, hospitable.
I want to be the sister who is never jealous, never
petty, and never small-minded.
I want to be the sister who never tears others
down, but instead builds up.
Lord, she's the perfect sister I want to be.

I want to be a friend, Lord, a neighbor to the
world . . .
Concerned, caring, and never too busy to help.
I want to be the friend who never gossips and
never competes.
I want to be the friend who sees the world
through Jesus' eyes, then cares enough to
change things.
Lord, she's the perfect friend I want to be.

I want to be a professional woman, Lord, a role
model for the young, but never at the expense
of her family . . .
Smart, successful, and competent.
I want to be the professional who achieves her goals
without forfeiting her ethics or her charm.
I want to be the professional who rises to the top,
but never loses sight of who she is and how
she got there.
Lord, she's the perfect professional woman I want
to be.

I want to be Your daughter, Lord, an honor to
Your name.
Simple, eager, and tender.
I want to be the daughter who never questions
Your wisdom and never doubts Your love.
I want to be the daughter who rests securely in
Your arms and wholly trusts Your leading.
Lord, she's the perfect daughter I want to be.

Someday I'll meet her, Lord, the wife and mother,
    the sister and friend—the woman I want to be.
She'll be wearing my freckles.
She'll be sporting my grin.
And she'll be lifting one eyebrow in whimsical
    disbelief.
Someday I'll turn around and there she'll be—
The perfect woman I want to be.

But until then, Lord, make me willing each day,
To be the woman *You* want me to be.
Anoint my eyes with compassion,
My ears with tolerance,
And my heart with joy.
Let me grow in Your grace.
Let my every word and my every deed be as
    pure and clear and transparent as sunlight.
May I live each moment to glorify Your
    holy name.
Lord, that's the kind of woman You can create
    in me.

Add more joy and meaning to your prayer life with Carrol Johnson Shewmake's books on prayer

Practical Pointers to Personal Prayer
Carrol Johnson Shewmake guides you step-by-step toward satisfying communion with your heavenly Father. She tells how she lost the boredom and guilt that choked her lifeline to God and instead found intimate two-way conversation. Paper, 128 pages.

Sanctuary Secrets to Personal Prayer
This book introduces you to a unique prayer experience that takes you through the steps performed by the priests in the Old Testament sanctuary. Paper, 92 pages.

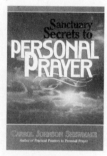

Sensing His Presence, Hearing His Voice
The author shows how you can cultivate hearing the voice of God and have a continual sense of His presence. Paper, 140 pages.

When We Pray for Others
The author helps you begin an intercessory prayer ministry and shows how it can bring greater joy and closeness to God. Ideal for individual or small group study. Paper, 128 pages.

US$7.99, Cdn$10.80 each.

The Incredible Answers to Prayer Series

by Roger Morneau

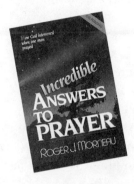 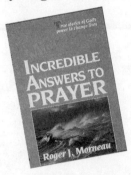 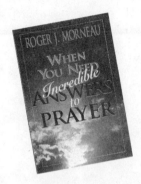

ROGER MORNEAU is a man of incredible faith. When he prays, things happen. And it's exciting! As a result, he's received thousands of letters and telephone calls from people requesting intercessory prayer. He shares many of those requests in this series along with God's thrilling answers.

He also shows how you can walk more closely with God, share His power and love with others, and receive incredible answers to prayer. Titles include *Incredible Answers to Prayer, More Incredible Answers to Prayer*, and *When You Need Incredible Answers to Prayer*.

Paper, US$7.99, Cdn$14.85 each.
Also available on video. US$39.95, Cdn$53.95 two-volume set.

My Beloved Son
The life of Christ through Mary's eyes

By Joan Krogstad Ireland

This is Mary's story--an intimate glimpse into her heart and soul, and the hopes and fears that lingered there for Jesus.

Her bittersweet memories paint vividly what it was like to raise a little boy who would someday save the world, to bathe and hold Him, to teach Him at her knee, to try to protect Him from a hatred she could not understand, and finally to let Him go, remembering He had always really belonged to Someone else.

Through her eyes we witness a very special relationship and see more clearly the matchless love of her Son.

Paper, 171 pages.
US$10.99, Cdn$14.85.

An Exciting New Way to Organize Your Prayer Life

Make your prayer life more meaningful with this creative new approach by Nancy Van Pelt. In *My Prayer Notebook* she helps you to focus on a specific type of prayer request each day of the week. For example, she suggests that you pray for yourself on Monday, your spouse on Tuesday, etc.

My Prayer Notebook will give you a way to organize your prayer requests and answers, and will deepen your faith in God as you see His leading in your life.

My Prayer Notebook includes

- ❧ A beautiful 3-ring binder to enhance your devotional time.
- ❧ 128 ruled pages for recording your prayer requests, sermon notes, Bible study notes, etc.
- ❧ Dividers for the days of week.
- ❧ Dividers for Bible study notes, answered prayer, sermon notes, favorite Scripture, plus two blanks.
- ❧ Instructions on how to personalize and use your prayer notebook.
- ❧ Tips on making personal devotion time more enjoyable.
- ❧ Creative ideas for Bible study.
- ❧ Refill sheets available.

US$17.99, Cdn$24.30.